Building Relationships with Parents and Families in School-Age Programs

2nd Edition, Revised

Resources for Staff Training and Program Planning

by Roberta L. Newman

originally published in conjunction with WFD Consulting

School-Age NOTES • New Albany, Ohio

Credits
Cover Photo: Michael Newman/PhotoEdit
Cover Design: Linda Sorrells-Smith, Sorrells-Smith Graphic Design
Illustrations: Paul Richmond
Book Design: David Pickard

School-Age
NOTES
Resources for AfterSchool Professionals

P.O. Box 476
New Albany, OH 43054
614-855-9315
www.SchoolAgeNotes.com

This book was originally excerpted and adapted from Roberta L. Newman's
Keys to Quality in School-Age Child Care Viewer's Guide and Trainer's Guide

ISBN-13: 978-0-917505-21-8

Table of Contents

Dedicated with love and affection to my parents,
Anna Ingeborg and Robert Emmanuel Liden

Preface to the 2nd Edition

The 2nd edition of *Building Relationships with Parents and Families* continues to emphasize that creating positive relationships with parents is the foundation for strong, ongoing partnerships between parents and programs. When parents are actively and positively involved in children's lives, children and youth benefit. Whether an out-of-school program is focused on enrichment, child and youth development, recreation, tutoring or some combination of all of these, connecting with parents is an important strategy for maximizing the benefits to children and youth.

Parents have a lot of important information, ideas, perspectives and insights to share about their children that can help staff become more effective with children. Program staff also have a lot of information, ideas, perspectives and insights about how children engage in program activities and interact with others in a group setting. When parents and program staff share their views, wonderful things can and do happen for kids. But sharing can only happen in an atmosphere of trust and respect. That's what *Building Relationships* is all about — exploring and using effective strategies and tools to develop trust and respect that lead to strong partnerships between parents and program staff. With this in mind, the 2nd Edition places a heavy emphasis on the importance of developing and using effective communication skills as a major tool for building relationships with parents.

As in the first edition, this book contains three major sections that include training activities, program tools, tip sheets and other ideas for connecting with parents. The changes to the 2nd Edition include revised and expanded learning activities and answer guides to reflect current issues and concerns; revised and expanded handouts; enhanced and expanded tools for assessing parent needs and concerns; new and expanded tip sheets for building connections with parents; and a selected reference list.

Positive relationships provide the cornerstone for connecting strong families, great programs and healthy communities. I sincerely hope this book will bring you much success as you work to build positive relationships with all the parents and families in your program!

Please stay in touch and share your ideas and successes with me! Send your news to me via e-mail at Newroads_Consulting@earthlink.net.

Roberta Newman

A Word About Technology and Relationship Building

This 2nd Edition of *Building Relationships with Parents and Families in School-Age Programs* provides extensive learning activities to help staff in school-age programs create positive relationships with parents and families. It also offers new and improved tools, tips and ideas that staff can use to strengthen and maintain productive partnerships between staff and parents. In addition, the 2nd Edition encourages the use of available technology (for example, e-mail, the Internet, webcams and so on) as tools for sharing information and increasing communication between staff and parents. As this book is published, it is important to acknowledge that new technological tools are emerging daily. It is likely that many new technologies will increase the speed and efficiency with which programs can get information to parents and vice versa.

As new technologies arrive on the scene, however, it is important for programs to think carefully about whether a new communication tool will enhance or detract from genuine communication. By all means, it is important to get critical information out to parents in the most efficient way possible. Technology is obviously a great tool for accomplishing information dissemination. At the same time, it is necessary to look carefully at what types of tools we use when we are committed to having genuine conversations that promote feedback and mutual understanding. When all is said and done, relationship building is a person-to-person endeavor. It requires human interaction and conversation. Use the new technologies that arrive on the scene to share important information. But, when your major focus is sharing and exploring ideas and concerns, building trust and promoting understanding, remember that personal, face-to-face human interaction is the most effective way to further your relationship-building goals.

Introduction

Strong, positive, cooperative relationships with parents and families are at the heart of quality out-of-school programs for school-age children and youth. Quality programs strive to work with parents as active partners who communicate regularly to share important ideas, news, feelings and concerns. The ways in which parents connect with programs may vary widely because of individual differences among parents and the ages of their children. But one thing is certain: When programs connect with parents in positive ways, elementary- and middle-school kids are more likely to grow and thrive through their out-of-school experiences.

Unfortunately, positive relationships with parents and families are not always easy to achieve because parents, like children, have widely varying personalities; some are easier to reach and connect with than others. Parents come from diverse backgrounds and have different ideas, values, concerns, knowledge, pressures, lifestyles, plans, dreams, resources and constraints. Staff who are successful in building positive relationships begin by recognizing the importance of accepting parents as the most important people in children's lives, regardless of differences among them.

In today's complex world, it is important to recognize that the traditional definitions and roles of parents have changed significantly and are continuing to change. In view of this, it is important for readers to know that the use of the word "parents" in this book is intended to be inclusive of all those who may be fulfilling the role of parent in the lives of children in your program. While many children in your program may live in traditionally defined two-parent families, many others may live in single-parent homes. Still others may live with a grandparent, an older sibling, an aunt or uncle, an adoptive parent, a foster parent or someone else who is temporarily assuming the parental role while a parent is away. The goal of this book is to help school-age staff reach out and connect with whomever is assuming the parental role(s) while a child is participating in your program. **As you use the training sessions and program tools, please keep in mind that references to "parents" include any adult who is fulfilling the role of primary caregiver for a child in your program.**

The one unifying theme among today's parents may be that many of them are stressed by the challenges of earning a living and fulfilling their obligations in the workplace while trying to build and maintain healthy relationships with the significant people in their personal lives — spouses, children, other family members, friends and significant others. Some parents have more capacities and skills for handling this balancing act successfully than others. The extent to which parents feel that their lives are manageable and under some degree of control has a strong influence on the extent to which they are able and willing to be resourceful partners with their children's out-of-school programs. In quality programs, accepting, supportive staff members help parents feel welcome and valued as partners. These programs recognize that school-age care and other out-of-school programs provide a family service and that parents and children are the clients or customers. They recognize that programs are not replacements for parents and that, in order to succeed with children, they must constantly reach out to parents. In these successful programs, staff take the initiative in relationship building. If things do not go well or there is no response from parents, staff assume that there are things they can do to alter the situation. If one thing is not working, staff vary their approach and try something else.

This book is designed to help program directors, trainers and staff develop a wide range of strategies and tools for connecting with parents who often have different wants, needs and concerns even when they come from similar backgrounds. The book is organized into three main sections:

1. **Section One:** Reaching Out to Parents as Partners
   (Learning Activities for Program Staff)

2. **Section Two:** Assessing the Needs, Interests and Concerns of Parents
   (Tools to Use in Your Program)

3. **Section Three:** Making Connections with Parents
   (Tip Sheets for Program Staff)

A brief overview of each section follows.

SECTION ONE: REACHING OUT TO PARENTS AS PARTNERS

Section One includes six **Core Learning Activities** designed to help staff improve their abilities to build positive relationships with parents. Trainer notes and handouts are provided for each activity. The **Learning Activities** are aimed at accomplishing the following goals:

- Help staff examine their own attitudes, beliefs and relationship-building skills

- Explore effective communication skills as the basic building blocks of relationship building

- Provide information about the stages of parenthood and pressures on parents; and explore diverse parental needs, interests and concerns

- Deepen staff members' understanding of parents — what they want and need

- Develop fresh approaches to building positive relationships and addressing problems and concerns with parents

- Develop a spirit of resourcefulness and resilience for responding effectively to parents' special needs, concerns and/or circumstances

SECTION TWO: ASSESSING THE NEEDS, INTERESTS AND CONCERNS OF PARENTS

Section Two provides a variety of tools for use in your program. It includes the following materials:

- Ideas for creating a family-friendly poster and sample posters
- Cover letters and forms for gathering information from parents about their children and about their own interests, needs and concerns
- Ideas for soliciting ongoing suggestions from parents
- Ideas for developing parent bulletin boards, Web sites and newsletters
- Sample parent survey forms

SECTION THREE: MAKING CONNECTIONS WITH PARENTS

Section Three recognizes differences among parents and offers tip sheets that encourage programs and staff to provide a variety of ways for parents to connect with programs. Tip sheets address the following topics:

- Helping parents feel welcome, accepted and valued
- Helping parents get to know program staff
- Providing parents with opportunities to help shape the program
- Helping parents get to know other parents and children in the program
- Helping parents support their child's school success
- Advocating on behalf of parents and families

Section Three also includes a concluding article *Building and Sustaining Positive Relationships with Parents.*

EXPANDING ON SECTIONS TWO AND THREE

The tools and tips in **Sections Two** and **Three** are intended to supplement and build on the learning activities presented in **Section One**. Depending upon the needs and focus of your program, you may want to use some of the materials from **Sections Two** and **Three** as the basis for designing additional training sessions of your own.

SELECTED REFERENCES

See the **Selected References** provided at the end of the book for a list of resources related to ideas and strategies presented in *Building Relationships with Parents and Families in School-Age Programs.*

Reaching Out to Parents as Partners
(Learning Activities for Program Staff)

Introduction to Section One

Section One includes six Core Learning Activities:

1. Examining Attitudes Toward Parents

2. Creating Positive Communication with Parents

3. Building Alliances with Parents of School-Age Children

4. Exploring Parent Roles

5. What Parents Want and Need from School-Age Programs

6. Responding to Parents with Special Concerns and Needs

Trainer notes, activity instructions and handouts for participants are provided for each learning activity. Some learning activities include *Optional Activity Instructions* for adapting the activity for different–sized groups. Some learning activities include a *Core Learning Activity* and a *Follow-Up Activity*.

As indicated in each *Learning Activity Overview*, learning activity segments require from thirty minutes to two hours and thirty minutes training time. Depending on the time available for staff training in your program, you may conduct each workshop at a separate session; combine learning activities for full-day training sessions; or separate single learning activities into smaller training segments on different days. The learning activities are designed to be flexible. Develop a schedule that fits your situation.

Examining Attitudes Toward Parents

PRELIMINARY NOTES

Experience has shown that staff often have widely varying attitudes toward parents. Even when programs provide parent-involvement training, these attitudes often go unacknowledged. This is unfortunate because staff views about parents can have strong positive or negative effects on your program's ability to develop plans for reaching out to parents effectively. Staff with positive attitudes tend to extend themselves and go the extra mile in building relationships with parents. On the other hand, negative preconceptions and attitudes toward parents can prevent staff from taking the initiative to build positive relationships with parents. With this in mind, **Core Learning Activity One** is designed to help staff identify their current attitudes toward parents and examine how these attitudes can enhance or detract from their ability to build positive relationships with parents. It encourages staff to identify, share and discuss current attitudes toward parents before developing strategies for building positive staff/parent relationships. As you conduct the learning activity, you may be surprised to discover how staff in your program view parents!

Activity Overview

(Optional Activity Instructions for the Core Learning Activity appear at the end of the *Large Group Discussion Questions and Summary of Teaching Points*)

Number of participants: 10 to 35

Trainer resources:
   Opinion statements
   Large Group Discussion Questions and
      Summary of Teaching Points

Handouts:
   CLA1-1 Opinion Statements (Distribute only
   if the Optional Activity Instructions are used)

CLA1-2 Small Group Discussion
   Questions (Distribute only if the
   Optional Instructions are used)

Time needed: 1 hour and 15 minutes

Space: An area large enough for participants to spread out along a "human continuum" as indicated in the instructions

CONDUCTING THE ACTIVITY

Use the following material to introduce the workshop to your staff. The statements in **BLUE** can be used as a "script" for introducing the activity. Additional notes, instructions or clarifications for the trainer appear in *ITALICS*. Be sure to set a relaxed, casual tone for the activity so that staff will feel comfortable revealing their feelings.

> In order for us to work effectively with children in out-of-school programs, it is very important for us to recognize and accept parents as partners with our programs. The attitudes and opinions we have about parents have a strong effect on our

ability to interact effectively with parents of children in our program. Sometimes those of us who work in programs develop opinions about parents that can make it difficult, if not impossible, to view parents as partners. As a first step toward developing good communication and positive relationships, it is important for us to acknowledge our feelings about parents of the children we serve and to discuss how these feelings can either help or hinder our work with families. We are going to do this through an activity where you will move from place to place based on your views on a series of statements I will share with you.

At this point, have participants move to an area where they can spread out in a line facing you. Once everyone has moved, proceed to give the instructions that follow.

The statements I will read are all direct quotes from staff working in a variety of out-of-school programs. Listen carefully to the exact wording and position yourself accordingly. After I read each statement, I would like you to position yourself from left to right along an imaginary line to indicate how you feel about the statement:

- Position yourself as far as possible to the **left** if you **strongly agree** with the statement.

- Position yourself as far as possible to the **right** if you **strongly disagree** with the statement.

- Position yourself somewhere in the **middle** if you have **mixed feelings** about the statement.

To choose your position, go with your immediate reactions to the statements, rather than reflecting on the pros and cons of each statement. After you position yourself for each statement, notice where you seem to share the same viewpoint as other colleagues as well as where you have differing opinions. After you have heard all of the statements, we will take some time to discuss our reactions and feelings and how they may affect our ability to build positive relationships with parents in your program.

Before proceeding, pause briefly to ask if there are any questions. When everyone is clear, read each opinion statement on **Handout CLA1-1,** *giving participants time to move along the continuum in response to each statement.*

It is very likely that staff will have varying attitudes about many of these statements. This will become evident as staff move themselves along the imaginary line to indicate their feelings. Sometimes this can be a real eye-opener as staff begin to realize that widely varying attitudes may be affecting their abilities to develop and sustain a consistent, positive team approach to building relationships with parents.

After participants have indicated their reactions to each statement, have everyone return to their seats. Facilitate a large group discussion using the **Large Group Discussion Questions and Summary of Teaching Points** *as a guide.*

CORE LEARNING ACTIVITY ONE

Opinion Statements

INSTRUCTIONS (FOR SMALL GROUP WORK)

The following statements are quotes from staff working in various out-of-school programs. Think about whether you agree or disagree with each statement. Talk with your colleagues and share your own feelings. Discuss your reaction to each statement exactly as it reads.

1. Most parents today just do not seem to have time for their children. All they want to do is get them in an after-school program and forget about them until it is time to go home. There is no way to get parents involved in programs.

2. When parents are too busy for their children, staff should try as hard as possible to be a substitute for the parent. After all, somebody needs to care!

3. Most parents are not interested in quality programming. They just want to know how much it costs and how long the program will be open.

4. To a child, a parent is the most important person in the world.

5. Most parents really want to be part of their children's lives. They just do not seem be able to make the time.

6. Many parents today do not seem to know a thing about raising children; as a result, children are always misbehaving.

7. At the end of the day, parents are in a hurry; they do not seem to care whether their children finish activities or help with clean-up.

8. Parents have many good ideas about how after-school programs should be run.

9. When children are having problems in a program, most parents do not want to hear about it.

10. Parents are a valuable resource for program planning.

LARGE GROUP DISCUSSION QUESTIONS AND SUMMARY OF TEACHING POINTS

LARGE GROUP DISCUSSION QUESTIONS

Suggestion: Post the opinion statements on chart paper for reference during discussion.

1. Which statements do staff members disagree on? What accounts for any differences of opinion?

2. Are there any statements on which there is unanimous agreement? If yes, what accounts for this?

3. Which statements do staff have strong opinions about? Discuss how these opinions might have an impact on the program's ability to develop a family-friendly atmosphere. For example:

   - Will any of the opinions enhance efforts to develop positive relationships with parents? If so, how?

   - Will any of the opinions hinder efforts to develop positive relationships with parents? If so, how?

   - How do negative or non-existent staff/parent relationships affect children? Staff? Parents?

   - Could we improve our staff/parent relationships just by adjusting our attitudes toward parents and changing our approach to them? Why or why not?

4. After listening to the discussion of the different opinion statements, have you changed your mind about your reactions to any of the statements? If yes, what accounts for the change?

5. We are all human; therefore, both parents and school-age professionals have values, beliefs, concerns and traditions that influence our attitudes and color the way we look at each other. When negative attitudes get in the way of professional behavior, however, the situation usually goes from bad to worse. Think about the following questions:

   - Do you think it is possible to have a quality out-of-school program without positive relationships between parents and staff? Why or why not?

   - What can we do to cope with attitudes in ourselves that may make it difficult to do our jobs effectively?

SUMMARY OF TEACHING POINTS

- Attitudes about parents can help or hinder the development of partnerships with parents. For example, after-school staff who believe parents just want to "enroll children in a program and forget about them" are not likely to make strong efforts to get parents involved. They have already decided parents are not interested. Staff who believe "most parents are not interested in quality programming" are not likely to spend much effort aimed at keeping parents informed about the program. On the other hand, staff who believe parents "have lots of good ideas about how an after-school program should be run" are likely to solicit parents' suggestions, ideas and concerns as a resource for improving the program. And staff who believe "to a child, a parent is the most important person in the world" are very likely to work hard at building positive relationships with parents that, in turn, can strengthen parent/child relationships.

- It is important to acknowledge that all of us have values, beliefs, concerns and traditions that influence our attitudes toward one another. In fact, most of us have very strong attachments to our attitudes and values. Witness a slogan seen on a bumper sticker: "I don't need your Attitude; I've got one of my own!" And yet, if we want to support children as part of a family, we cannot afford the luxury of ignoring the attitudes of others or how our own attitudes may be affecting our ability to establish positive relationships with parents.

- Sometimes, even our best efforts to reach parents do not yield the results we are looking for. When we are unable to create positive relationships despite our best efforts, it may be time to ask for help from a supervisor or an experienced colleague, or secure assistance from others in the community with special knowledge and expertise in building relationships in challenging situations (for example, counselors, health professionals, social workers and so on).

Optional Activity Instructions

If the group is larger than thirty-five, you may want to break participants up into small groups of five or six to compare their reactions to the statements. If you do this, use the following steps to conduct the activity:

- *Provide each small group with a set of the* **opinion statements (Handout CLA1-1)** *and* **Small Group Discussion Questions (Handout CLA1-2).**

- *Have each group select a leader to read the statements and lead small group discussion.*

- *Allow twenty to thirty minutes for small group discussion of participant reactions to each statement using the discussion questions.*

- *Bring the groups together for sharing. Have the leader from each group share the results of their group discussion.*

- *Facilitate a large group discussion, using the* **Large Group Discussion Questions and Summary of Teaching Points,** *as a guide.*

Note: By adding time for small group work, you may need additional time for this session. The physical movement of participants as they indicate their opinions usually takes only five to ten minutes, whereas breaking into small groups will require twenty-five to thirty minutes to allow group members to share their opinions through discussion.

For groups smaller than ten, you may want to discuss each statement informally rather than having staff move physically to indicate their positions or divide into even smaller groups.

CORE LEARNING ACTIVITY ONE

Small Group Discussion Questions

INSTRUCTIONS:

Use these questions to discuss and share your responses to the opinion statements on **Handout CLA1-1** distributed to your small group.

1. Which statements do staff members disagree on? What accounts for any differences of opinion?

2. Are there any statements about which there is unanimous agreement? If yes, what accounts for this?

3. Which statements do group members have strong opinions about? Discuss how these opinions might have an impact on a program's ability to develop a family-friendly atmosphere. For example:

   - Will any of the opinions enhance efforts to develop positive relationships with parents? If so, how?

   - Will any of the opinions hinder efforts to develop positive relationships with parents? If so, how?

   - How do negative or non-existent staff/parent relationships affect children? Staff? Parents?

   - Could we improve our staff/parent relationships just by adjusting our attitudes toward parents and changing our approach to them? Why or why not?

Using Positive Attitudes Toward Parents to Create a Family-Friendly Atmosphere

PRELIMINARY NOTES

As staff have discovered in **Core Learning Activity One**, negative attitudes often can distract us from building positive relationships with parents. Even when we recognize that our negative attitudes are getting in the way, it can be difficult to change long-standing or deeply held negative attitudes into positive ones. This **Follow-Up Activity** gives staff an opportunity to explore ways to open and stretch their minds and transform negative attitudes into positive ones that can strengthen partnerships with parents.

Activity Overview

Number of participants: Any number, working in groups of two or three

Trainer resources:
Chart pad and marker (for posting brainstorming questions and responses)

Core Learning Activity One Follow-Up Activity Answer Guide

Handout:
CLA1-3 Using Positive Attitudes Toward Parents to Create a Family-Friendly Atmosphere

Time needed: 30 to 45 minutes (or more if ideas are developed beyond brainstorming stage)

Space: An area appropriate for participants to work at tables in small groups

---

CONDUCTING THE ACTIVITY

Use the following material to introduce the activity to your staff. The statements in BLUE can be used as a "script" for introducing the activity. Additional notes, instructions or clarifications for the trainer appear in *ITALICS*.

Negative attitudes can be difficult to change, even when we recognize they are not working for us. Let us brainstorm some possible answers to the questions I have posted:

- How can you work on changing attitudes that get in your way?

- What are some strategies you can use to change a negative attitude when you know it is not working for you?

List participant responses on chart paper. Then discuss any of the following strategies not already cited by staff during brainstorming.

- Acknowledge negative attitudes and make a commitment to thinking outside the box to expand your view of a person or situation. Open your mind to new ideas and possibilities (for example, ask: "How would I feel if I was in that person's situation?")

- Try stating things from someone else's perspective (for example, argue a position that is different from your own).

- Adopt a positive attitude for a specified period of time. Require yourself to act on the positive attitude until the time period is over. Then ask yourself whether your adopted attitude opened new possibilities for you.

- Try role-playing how you would act or what you would do if your attitude was positive rather than negative.

After discussing some ways to work on negative attitudes that hinder staff efforts at relationship building, provide staff with copies of **Using Positive Attitudes Toward Parents to Create a Family-Friendly Atmosphere (Handout CLA1-3).** *Tell staff this activity is designed to help them explore ways to transform negative attitudes into positive ones and generate new, fresh ideas for building partnerships with parents. Review instructions on the handout and have staff work on the assignment in groups of two or three between sessions. Or, conduct the* **Follow-Up Activity** *during the same session, immediately after completing the* **Core Learning Activity.**

After staff complete small group work, reconvene the larger group to share ideas. Use the **Answer Guide** *for* **Core Learning Activity One Follow-Up Activity** *to facilitate discussion.*

CORE LEARNING ACTIVITY ONE FOLLOW-UP ACTIVITY

Using Positive Attitudes Toward Parents to Create a Family-Friendly Atmosphere

INSTRUCTIONS

Work with a partner (or small group) to review the *Positive Attitude Statements* below. Identify at least two statements that you think could be very important but are not too evident in yourself or in your colleagues. Then, stretch your mind and work with your partner(s) to develop a list of at least five family-friendly actions that you and your program could take in relation to each statement. As you work together, identify specific things that you could say or do that would let parents know that you support the positive attitude statements you have chosen. If time allows, select one of your best ideas for each statement and make a plan to implement it in your program.

POSITIVE ATTITUDE STATEMENTS

1. Most parents want to know that their children are safe, happy, productive, valued as individuals and well cared for in after-school programs.

2. To a child, a parent is the most important person in the world.

3. Even though they are often pressed for time, most parents really want to be part of their children's lives in after-school programs.

4. Most parents would like to know more about helping their children make friends and get along well with other people.

5. Parents have many good ideas about how a child-care program should be run.

6. When their children are having problems in child care, most parents want to know what they can do to help solve the problems.

7. Parents have many interesting talents, hobbies and skills to share.

8. Parents have a wealth of important knowledge to share about their children's interests, talents, concerns, strengths and weaknesses.

9. Many parents would like to follow up on school-age program activities with their children at home.

CORE LEARNING ACTIVITY ONE FOLLOW-UP ACTIVITY

Answer Guide

Here are some family-friendly actions staff might take if they acted on each positive attitude statement.

POSITIVE ATTITUDE STATEMENTS AND RELATED FAMILY-FRIENDLY ACTIONS

1. **Most parents want to know that their children are safe, happy, productive, valued as individuals and well cared for in after-school programs.**

   - Create brochures, posters and pamphlets that describe and illustrate all the ways the program supports, protects and enriches children's lives.

   - Create an attractive parent bulletin board with a lot of information about program activities and events.

   - Develop a regular parent newsletter that includes interesting descriptions of children's experiences in the program.

   - Share photos of children's program experiences on the parent bulletin board and in a program scrapbook.

   - Develop portfolios with individual children that document their work and play in the program through photos, written observations and children's work samples.

2. **To a child, a parent is the most important person in the world.**

   - Create a system to encourage children to share their accomplishments with parents.

   - Invite parents to participate in program activities with their children — even if it is just for a few minutes at the end of the day.

   - Invite parents to share their family traditions; incorporate family traditions in program activities and experiences.

   - Set up a center where children can create greeting cards and gifts for their parents at any time.

   - Plan talent shows, family nights and other special activities where children and parents can enjoy time working and playing together.

3. **Even though they are often pressed for time, most parents really want to be part of their children's lives in after-school programs.**

   - Invite parents to spend a few minutes with their children at pickup time.

   - Ask parents to collect recyclables or donate other materials for use in the program.

   - Investigate the use of a webcam that would allow parents to check in on their children during the program day.

- Invite parents to help create a special interest club or special event.

- Invite parents to help plan and/or attend a field trip.

4. **Most parents would like to know more about helping their children make friends and get along well with other people.**

    - Conduct objective observations of children's interactions with others and share observations with parents on a regular basis.

    - Share anecdotes and quotes from children in action with parents to help them learn more about how their children interact with others.

    - Set up a display of magazine articles and books related to developing social skills near the parent bulletin board.

    - Plan and host a parent education series where parents learn about fostering their children's social development.

    - Develop a "Social Graces" club in the program and share club experiences with parents (for example, host a tea party or dance; plan a performance of courtesy skits or good sports role-plays; publish a kids' etiquette book; and so on).

5. **Parents have many good ideas about how a child-care program should be run.**

    - Set up a parent suggestion box and implement great ideas.

    - Conduct regular parent satisfaction surveys.

    - Invite parents to give feedback about existing program activities and experiences.

    - Host regular parent meetings that include time for parents to share their ideas.

    - Set up a parent advisory board and involve parents in creating initiatives and solving problems.

6. **When their children are having problems in child care, most parents want to know what they can do to help solve the problems.**

    - Have regular informal conversations and formal conferences with parents to share information about their children's experiences in the program.

    - Make objective observations of children and share written documentation of observations with parents.

    - Share ideas for helping children who are experiencing problems and encourage parents to share their own perspectives on what works and what does not work.

    - Post articles about common problems on the parent bulletin board.

    - Maintain and share a list of resource people and organizations that can provide support to children and parents who are experiencing problems.

7. **Parents have many interesting talents, hobbies and skills to share.**

   - Conduct a survey to learn about parents' talents, hobbies and skills.

   - Have regular conversations with children to learn about what parents enjoy doing in their spare time.

   - Post "Help Wanted" notices in the parent newsletter and/or parent bulletin board. (For example, "Does anyone specialize in Cajun cooking?" or "Could anyone help us string and tune our new guitar?")

   - Invite parents to post business cards on the parent bulletin board; invite parents to give presentations to children about their work.

   - Invite parents to join staff to put on a talent show.

8. **Parents have a wealth of important knowledge to share about their children's interests, talents, concerns, strengths and weaknesses.**

   - Develop a form where parents share information and insights about their children when they enroll.

   - Conduct telephone interviews with parents to learn more about children.

   - Invite parents to share information and insights about their children during parent conferences.

   - Develop a habit of asking parents about their children's experiences outside the program.

   - Take a systematic approach to asking parents to keep you informed about any changes in children's lives (for example, newsletter notices, posters, bulletin board notices).

9. **Many parents would like to follow up on school-age program activities with their children at home.**

   - Provide special snack recipes that parents and children can share at home.

   - Provide portable tape recorders and tapes for parents to record children's favorite stories or songs at home and share the recordings in the program library.

   - Send home directions for children's favorite program activities to try at home, and provide directions for special projects families can do at home together to follow up on program activities.

   - Suggest books or places to visit in the community where children and their families can learn more about ideas explored during program activities.

   - Videotape children participating in program activities and invite parents to check out the videos for viewing at home.

Creating Positive Communication with Parents

PRELIMINARY NOTES

Effective communication is the basis for all relationship building. Without effective communication, we cannot initiate or sustain positive relationships. And we certainly cannot work through problems when the going gets tough. Too often we think of communication as getting our point across. When we maintain this communication stance, it is difficult, if not impossible, to create mutual understanding. Defending our point of view prevents us from listening to ideas and concerns that are different from our own. It forces us into a win/lose strategy as we become more and more concerned with holding our ground rather than trying to broaden our understanding of a situation or problem.

Good communication involves give and take — constant feedback among the participants. As Douglas Stone puts it in his book *Difficult Conversations*, it is important to approach communication from the perspective of having a "learning conversation."* When we engage in *learning conversations*, we shift our agenda away from defending our own point of view. Instead, we embrace an agenda that is committed to *learning* what the other person is trying to say and helping our partner in conversation *learn* about what we are trying to say. This helps us suspend our judgments, expand our views and deepen our understanding. When we can do this, we are in a much better position to build strong partnerships and to solve problems. It is true that sometimes we have positions that cannot be changed because they are rooted in program policy, regulations or laws. Having a learning conversation does not require us to surrender our policies or regulations. We may have to hold firm to them in the end. But if we have had a civil, polite, reciprocal learning conversation, we are much more likely to come to a better understanding of issues in relation to the need for "compliance" than we would have if we simply issued a one-way statement that disallowed feedback.

Finally, effective communicators know that it is important to keep the communication channels open on a regular basis. It is not enough to learn how to communicate when problems occur. Regular give-and-take through positive communication builds trust and respect that makes it possible for us to have useful give-and-take when difficulties arise.

Core Learning Activity Two: Creating Positive Communication with Parents focuses on helping staff identify and practice effective communication techniques as they respond to parent questions and concerns.

---

* Stone, Douglas; Patton, Bruce; Heen, Sheila (all of the Harvard Negotiation Project); *Difficult Conversations: How to Discuss What Matters Most*. New York, New York: Penguin Group, Penguin Putnam, Inc. 1999.

Activity Overview

(See *Optional Activity Instructions* for groups of less than 6 at the end of Training Segment #3)

Number of participants: Any number of 6 and more

Handouts:

CLA2-1 Secrets of Good Communication

CLA2-2 "What If" Role Play Situations ... Are You Family Friendly?

Time needed: 1 hour and 15 minutes (15 minutes for introducing the activity,

25 minutes for communication role-play practice, 35 minutes for role-play demonstrations/discussion

Space: An area that allows for participants to spread out and work in pairs to practice communication role-plays, and space for demonstrating role-plays to the larger group

CONDUCTING THE ACTIVITY

This learning activity is divided into three segments. Use the Trainer Notes for each segment to facilitate workshop activities. The statements in BLUE can be used as a "script" for introducing the activity. Additional notes, instructions or clarifications for the trainer appear in *ITALICS*.

Trainer Notes for Segment #1: Exploring Communication Basics

As we discovered in Learning Activity One, positive attitudes and a problem-solving mindset are valuable qualities as we work to develop positive relationships with the families we serve. To create a family-friendly atmosphere, we need to build on these qualities by using effective communication skills. Let us take a moment to review what we know about good communication techniques.

Take fifteen minutes to discuss the following questions. Use the **Secrets of Good Communication (Handout CLA2-1)** *and the* Preliminary Notes *for* **Learning Activity Two** *as a tool for guiding the discussion. After the discussion, distribute the handout as a resource for participants.)*

Ask participants:

1. What is the purpose of communication?

2. How do we communicate with one another?

   • How does the communication process work?

   • What do we do when we listen?

   • What is the difference between passive and active listening?

3. What are some of the barriers to listening effectively to other people?

4. What are some strategies for being a good listener and preventing a communication breakdown?

CORE LEARNING ACTIVITY TWO

Secrets of Good Communication

1. **Why do we communicate?**

   A. To <u>share</u> our thoughts, ideas, feelings, values, perspectives and opinions and help others understand them

   B. To <u>learn</u> about the thoughts, ideas, feelings, values, perspectives and opinions of others

   C. To establish connections with other people

   D. To work with others to solve problems and conflicts

   E. To promote and deepen understanding of ourselves in relation to others

   F. Other?

2. **How do we communicate?**

   A. The communication process involves three components:

      1) The **sender** of the message

      2) The **message**

      3) The **receiver** of the message

   Communication begins when a sender states a message that is heard by the receiver. Next, the receiver must have an opportunity to respond to the message received (to give feedback). When this happens, the original sender becomes the new receiver. This launches a loop of feedback where each participant takes turns being the sender and receiver. Genuine communication happens when participants engage in giving and receiving continuous feedback as messages are exchanged and explored.

   B. Listening is a critical communication skill. There are three components to the effective listening process:

      1) **Hearing** the message.

      2) **Understanding** the message.

      3) **Remembering** the message.

   C. Effective listeners use a variety of communication skills that help them **hear, understand** and **remember** the messages they receive and exchange. There are two major types of listening: 1) **passive listening** and 2) **active listening.** Each type is associated with different types of listening skills and techniques.

      1) **Passive listening** uses attentive silence and minimal responses, either verbal ("I see." "Oh." "Uh-huh.") or nonverbal (nodding head slightly up and down or side to side; raising eyebrows slightly; frowning; smiling.) While passive listening can provide encouragement (or discouragement) to the sender of a message,

it does little to extend and expand the conversation in a way that promotes mutual understanding.

2) **Active listening:** Uses the ability to empathize with others. Active listening involves demonstrating to the other person that you understand what the other person expressed by *mirroring* or *interpreting the message back to that person.* This promotes continuous two-way feedback. Some examples of *active listening* techniques and skills to use in responding to a message:

Clarifying: *"I don't understand what you mean. Please explain that again."*

Paraphrasing or restating: *"This is what I think you mean.... Is that the idea?"*

Reflecting feelings: *"You seem to feel.... Am I right about that?"*

Summarizing main ideas and feelings: *"Here is what I've heard you say so far…"*

With practice, each of these active listening techniques can help us become better listeners and better communicators as we improve our ability to hear, understand and remember the messages we receive.

3. What are some of the barriers to being an effective listener?

Many factors can make it difficult to be an effective listener. Some of them are *external barriers.* Examples of external barriers to effective listening might be an uncomfortable or unwelcoming environment, noise distractions, lack of privacy, lack of time and so on. Other barriers to being an effective listener are related to *internal barriers* (how we think and feel about the world around us). Usually it is easier to eliminate external barriers than it is to eliminate internal barriers. Some examples of how our own internal attitudes and thoughts can become barriers to listening effectively and being an effective communicator:

A. Our **perceptions** of how things are (how we view the world around us) …
   - can make it difficult to look at things from different perspectives — from other peoples' points of view.
   - can make it difficult to empathize with others or to appreciate their feelings.

B. Our **opinions and beliefs** about what is right and what is wrong…
   - can lead us to make advance judgments about other people or situations, rather than listening to what they have to say.
   - can lead us to defend our own position, no matter what!
   - can lead us to rationalize our negativity, to self-justify or make excuses for negative attitudes or behavior.
   - can lead us to interrupt others before they've expressed their views.

C. Our **values** about what is important and what is not important…
   - can lead us to discount or dismiss what other people value.
   - can lead us to ignore what others have to say.

D. Our **negative attitudes or biases** toward certain individuals or groups (acknowledged or unacknowledged prejudices)…..

- can prevent us from tuning in to what people are saying.

- can lead us to ignore or dismiss the beliefs, values, needs, concerns, interests and rights of others.

- can lead us to exert our own power and influence to the detriment of others.

E. Other barriers?

4. **What are some effective strategies for being an effective communicator and preventing communication breakdown?**

A. Communicate in person whenever possible.

Telephones and e-mail are great resources for staying in touch and sharing information. However, neither of these devices is a substitute for genuine communication. Person-to-person communication allows participants in a conversation to see facial expressions or sense body language that helps them tune in to what the other person thinks and feels. Whenever possible, arrange to talk in person about important issues and concerns.

B. Create a positive listening environment.

Eliminate distractions and barriers (for example, go to a quiet place and avoid placing desks or tables between you and the other person unless you want to maintain a distant feeling or a power stance). Welcome your partner in conversation by exchanging pleasant greetings before the conversation begins.

C. Maintain eye contact when appropriate.

In Western culture, people often equate trustworthiness with looking someone in the eye. However, there are cultures around the world, including Native American, that view looking someone in the eye as a sign of disrespect. There are also individuals who are shy or withdrawn and find it uncomfortable to maintain eye contact. Learn as much as you can about the cultures and personal styles of parents in your program so that you can tune in to their preferred communication styles.

D. Avoid negative body language or facial expressions unless you think they truly promote understanding.

Folded arms can communicate that you are unapproachable, unwilling to listen or unwilling to yield power or position. Finger tapping can communicate impatience or nervousness. Frowning can communicate displeasure or confusion. Smirking can communicate contempt, ridicule or arrogance.

E. Use simple, direct language.

Most of what we want to share with parents can be communicated with simple, direct language. There is usually no need to use professional jargon (for example, specialized words relating to child development or programming research) when communicating with parents. For example, the statement "I'd like to discuss behavioral checklists and anecdotal records that demonstrate Joe's progress in developing social competencies" establishes distance between you and the parent who may not be familiar with these terms and may be intimidated by the formality of the statement. A more effective message would be: "I'd like to share some of my observations of Joe's interactions with other children in the program with you; I think you'll find them interesting and encouraging."

F. Motivate yourself to listen.

Identify and reflect on any internal barriers that may prevent you from being an effective listener and communicator. Do what you can to reduce the impact of these barriers. Then do your best to be attentive during conversations by keeping the following tips in mind as you communicate:

- It is impossible to *talk AND listen at the same time.*

- You cannot *plan what to say next AND listen at the same time.*

- Use self talk (messages you say silently to yourself) to help you use good communication techniques (for example, "Let her finish; don't interrupt." "Stay calm." "Listen for his main message." "Be kind.")

G. Motivate yourself to participate appropriately.

- Hold up your part of the conversation. Take an active role in exploring ideas and promoting understanding.

- Take turns talking. Avoid monopolizing the conversation.

- Avoid interrupting.

- Stay on the topic.

- If you want to change the subject, tell the other person you want to do so.

H. Be sensitive to emotions.

Difficult conversations can be charged with emotions. Do your best to maintain an atmosphere of respect. Try to become aware of your own emotional deaf spots (emotions that you are not willing to acknowledge in yourself or others). Some tips for communicating when emotions are running high:

- Hear emotions out. Avoid cutting them off. Rather than trying to stifle emotions, allow them to be expressed. Unexpressed emotions can boil over.

- Try to tune in and politely acknowledge the emotions behind the other person's words. (for example, "I can see that you feel very strongly about what you're saying. I'll do my best to understand your opinion.")

- Stay objective.

  - React to the message, not the person.

  - Withhold judgment and criticism.

  - Try not to escalate the other person's anger by responding with anger yourself.

I. Take notes if important data is too confusing, complicated or lengthy to commit to memory.

When people are angry or upset, communication often becomes muddled with accusations or disjointed comments. In this case, it can be very helpful to slow down the pace of the conversation by taking notes. Politely tell the person that you want to remember the important things they are saying and ask them to repeat what they've said so that you can write it down accurately. This accomplishes several things:

- It helps people think before they speak and focus on important points.

- It lets people know their ideas and feelings are being heard and taken seriously.

- It encourages people to state their points respectfully because they know their words are being written down.

J. Do not talk when you are too busy or distracted. Set up a special time to talk instead.

Trainer Notes for Segment #2: Communication Role-Play Practice

Before conducting the role-play practice and demonstrations in Training Segments 2 and 3, read the following comments about facilitating role-plays:

*Some staff may feel uncomfortable doing role-playing activities for a variety of reasons. For example, they may be shy or they may feel afraid they won't say the right thing. This activity is designed to help staff feel more comfortable and warm up to the role-play by working with a partner to practice. Role-play the **Situations** in two ways (one family unfriendly and one family friendly). A few additional comments about this activity:*

- *Sometimes staff have resentment toward parents (or other aspects of their job) that get in the way of responding to parents in a positive way. Staff who are allowed to express family-unfriendly responses and feelings in the role-plays are more likely to be open to thinking about how to develop a more family-friendly approach. This builds on principles of good communication that hold that we are more likely to solve problems and establish relationships with others if we are allowed to acknowledge our feelings. While we do not want negative feelings to surface during interactions with parents, it can be helpful to allow expression of these feelings in a safe training environment.*

- *Participants may feel shy about presenting role-plays in front of others, especially the role-play in which they are trying to use a family-friendly approach and have a learning conversation. Set a positive tone to encourage volunteers to get the role-play-session started:*

  - *Create a relaxed, comfortable atmosphere for this activity by encouraging staff to be playful and creative with the role-plays.*

  - *Emphasize the idea that effective communication is a skill. The more we practice communication skills, the more effective we become. As we practice any skill, we make mistakes — this is part of learning! Emphasize that role-playing is simply an opportunity to practice effective communication skills. No one is expected to give a perfect performance of family-friendly responses. The more we practice, the better we get at communicating effectively.*

  - *As staff give their role-play demonstrations, be sure to give supportive comments after each role-play version intended to portray a family friendly approach.*

Keep these points in mind as you introduce the training for Segment #2.

Use the following material to introduce the workshop to your staff. The statements in BLUE can be used as a "script" for introducing the activity. Additional notes, instructions or clarifications for the trainer appear in *ITALICS*.

> Now that we have reviewed some of the things we can do to communicate effectively with others, let us try to apply these strategies to our relationships with the parents in our program. To do this, we will work in pairs and do some role-playing.

Divide the group into pairs. If there is an uneven number of participants, invite one of the participants to be your partner for the activity. Then, distribute the handout **"What If"** **Role-Play Scenarios ... Are You Family Friendly? (Handout CLA2-2)** and continue with the instructions.

I am going to assign each set of partners two situations quoting comments that might be made by parents in our program.

Assign situations now. You may want to select one of the situations from the handout and talk through it with the larger group before partners begin to work together.

First take a few minutes with your partner to discuss possible staff responses to each situation assigned to you. Talk about how you might communicate under the following two conditions:

1. You were **not concerned** about giving a family-friendly response to the parent, but **were primarily concerned** with getting your own point across.

2. You were **committed** to giving a family-friendly response and having a learning conversation with the parent.

Then, work with your partner to role-play both situations assigned to you. For the first situation, have one partner play the role of the parent and the other play the role of a staff member. Switch roles for the second situation. As you role-play each situation, follow these guidelines:

*   Role-play two versions for each **situation**. In Version 1, have the designated staff member communicate as if she/he is **not concerned** about giving a family-friendly response or having a learning conversation. In Version 2, have the same staff member respond to the same parent comment as if he/she was **committed** to giving a family-friendly response and having a learning conversation.

*   As you participate in the role-plays, be sure to keep the conversation going with comments between the parent and the staff member and see where the conversation leads in each version.

*   As you role-play the versions where you are committed to having a learning conversation, try to keep in mind what we discussed about the importance of accepting parents in Core Learning Activity One as well as our discussion about effective communication techniques.

Pause and ask if there are any questions before partners begin to role-play.

We will work in pairs for about twenty minutes to practice our role-plays; then, we will reconvene, present the role-plays to the larger group and discuss the differences between the two versions of each role-play situation. Have fun!

"What If" Role-Play Situations ... Are You Family Friendly?

INSTRUCTIONS

The following comments are typical of those expressed by parents of children in school-age programs from time to time. Work with your partner to role-play both situations. For the first situation, have one partner play the role of the parent and the other play the role of a staff member. Switch roles for the second situation. As you role-play, follow these guidelines:

- Role-play two versions for each situation. In Version 1, have the designated staff member communicate as if she/he is not concerned about giving a family-friendly response or having a learning conversation. In Version 2, have the same staff member respond to the same parent comment as if he/she is committed to giving a family-friendly response and having a learning conversation. In both versions, have the parent speak first, using the situation as a start-up script.

- As you participate in the role-plays (both versions), be sure to keep the conversation going with comments back and forth between the parent and the staff member and see where the conversation leads.

- As you role-play the version where you are committed to having a learning conversation, try to keep in mind what we discussed about the importance of accepting parents in Learning Activity One as well as our discussion about effective communication techniques.

Situations ... How would you communicate with a parent who says:

1. "Whenever I come in here, none of the children seem to be doing anything productive ... they're all just playing around. I don't want my child wasting time playing when he's here or he'll never get ahead in life. I want him to learn something after school, not just hang out with his friends."

2. "When I pick Sharon up, I want her homework done, and I'm holding you responsible for that. By the time we get home in the evening, I'm totally exhausted and don't have time to help. Besides, Sharon wants to watch TV with the family after supper, not do homework."

3. "If Aaron gives you any trouble, lay down the law. We don't take any back talk from him. You can give him a swat if you want to. That's what works at home."

4. "Molly really needs to play outside after school. We live in an apartment where there's no place for her to play outside and there are no other children to play with indoors. Molly said she's not allowed to go outside or talk after school. She says she has to sit quietly at a table for the first forty-five minutes of the program because everyone has

to do homework. I don't want her to do her homework here — I like helping her in the evenings when we finish dinner. So please, let her go outside when she gets here. She needs the fresh air and time to play with her friends.

5. "Julie says the other kids make fun of her and call her a baby. Apparently, there are a lot of mean kids here, and they won't let Julie play with them. I'm really worried about her because this is the first year she's had to go to a day-care program. She says she doesn't want to come here any more and that she wants me to quit work so she can come home after school. I wish I could stay home, but I can't. I have to work. I don't know what to do because Julie cries every day when she leaves for kindergarten. She doesn't want to go there either."

6. "Don't tell me Damon has behavior problems. We have no problems with him at home. He works on the computer by himself for hours at a time, and he and his brother never give us any trouble. There must be something wrong with the program if you cannot get him to behave himself."

7. "Sarah is always complaining that the program is boring. She's been coming to the program for years, and she's tired of the same old activities. The camp she went to over the summer had all sorts of interesting clubs for the kids like cooking, magic, photography, computers and jazz dance. She was so enthused about it. Here, it is either do the daily art activity, play outside or do your homework. Isn't there something you could do to make things more interesting?"

8. "Kim said he's afraid to come to the program lately. He says some of the older boys have threatened him during the program and told him if he doesn't do what they tell him to do, their gang will hurt him or his younger brother. How can you let kids act like that in the program? Don't you have any control?"

9. "Casey never used bad words until he started coming to this program. Now he uses four-letter words whenever he gets angry at home. And he uses racial slurs that we don't allow in our family. Casey says everybody thinks Derek is cool and that he wants to be like Derek. He says Derek always swears and calls people names. I want to talk with Derek's parents about this, and I want you to give me their phone number."

10. "Kenny has started playing with some kids from a bad neighborhood while he's here. Those kids don't have any manners, and I'm afraid Kenny will pick up bad habits. I want you to keep Kenny away from them."

11. "You say Tanisha is rude to the staff in the program? Well, it doesn't surprise me. She drives me crazy at home, too. I can't get her to do anything I ask her to do. All she wants to do is talk on her cell phone and listen to her CDs. She needs to help out around the house, but she won't. She says her friends don't have to do chores at home. I guess I made a mistake sending her to this program because she seems to be getting a real attitude from the other kids. She was never this rude 'til she came here."

12. "It seems to me that the older kids rule in this program. When I pick up Ricky, I've noticed some of the older kids picking on him and some of the other little kids. Can't you divide the program into groups of older and younger kids? I think you should keep the older kids away from the younger ones."

13. "I know I'm late again. My boss just won't let me leave until 5:30 P.M. If I make all the lights, I can get here by 6:00 P.M. But half the time, there's some sort of traffic jam that costs me ten or fifteen minutes. Can't you be more understanding? If I leave fifteen minutes early, I could get fired. But, your five dollar late charge is also killing me. Gary is such a sweet kid; I'm sure he doesn't cause you any trouble while he waits for me. Can't you just be a little flexible and waive the fee? I'm not a deadbeat who is late because she stops to go shopping. I just have no alternatives. The only other center that stays open later is fifteen minutes further out of my way, and their fees are higher than yours."

14. "This place is so disorganized! When I come to get Keisha, I have to spend ten minutes hunting her down. She could be outside, in the art area, in the gym or playing board games. I never know where to find her. And what's worse, I can't find any staff to help me; everybody's busy doing something. I have a really tight schedule, and I don't like having to track Keisha down when I get here. Can't you just have her stay in one place after 5:00 P.M.? I'm usually here by 5:30; I don't think it would hurt her to pack up and wait quietly until I get here."

15. "It's great to have an after-school program, but I work on Saturdays, too. Couldn't you offer a special Saturday program?"

16. "I don't know what I'm going to do if you close early for bad weather some day. I just won't be able to get here until the regular closing time. I'll bet there are other parents who will be in the same boat. You need to stay open later to help us out."

Trainer Notes for Segment #3: Role-Play Demonstrations and Discussion

Use the following questions to guide follow-up discussions as each set of role-plays is presented and to wrap up the training activity.

1. How did the communication techniques used affect the outcome of each role-play?

2. What were some of the differences between the family-friendly role-play versions and the "not family-friendly" role-plays? How did these differences affect the relationships between the staff and the parent in the role-plays? For example:

   - Did you hear responses that acknowledged the feelings or emotions of parents? If yes, what were they? If not, what could have been said?

   - Why is it important to acknowledge feelings and emotions?

     - How does it help the parent?

     - How does it help the staff person?

     - How does it help build relationships between staff and parents?

3. What are the most important communication skills we need to develop in order for our program to be more "family friendly?" In addition to ongoing role-playing practice, what are some other ways we could work together to improve our communication skills? *(Possible answers: problem solving actual situations in the program, readings on the topic, observing colleagues with good communication skills, working with a mentor or partner to observe and critique each other's communication skills.)*

4. Why do you think it might be easier to talk about problems with parents if you have worked to build an ongoing relationship with them? *(Possible answer: relationships help build trust, respect and confidence among people — it is easier to discuss difficult issues with someone you know and trust.)*

Optional Activity Instructions

Assigning the Role-Plays for Small Groups ...

- *For groups smaller than six, discuss and practice each role-play situation as a whole group, rather than working with partners.*

- *For groups of six to twelve participants, consider assigning three or four role-plays to each set of partners. Expand the amount of time allowed for practice with partners; reduce the amount of time allowed for large group discussion accordingly.*

Note: Consider providing ongoing opportunities for staff to practice good communication skills through role-playing activities. Allow fifteen minutes for communication skill building at regular staff meetings. Create additional role-play situations based on experiences in your program.

CORE LEARNING ACTIVITY THREE

Building Alliances with Parents of School-Age Children

PRELIMINARY NOTES

The first two learning activities focused on helping staff develop and build on positive attitudes toward parents and learn strategies for communicating effectively with parents. When staff make improvements in these areas, they are much more likely to build strong, lasting alliances with parents. This learning activity focuses on learning and using effective problem solving strategies that can further improve our ability to build and sustain positive relationships with parents.

In **Core Learning Activity Three:** *Building Alliances with Parents of School-Age Children*, staff learn and apply a step-by-step approach to problem solving as they explore ways to work through difficult and challenging situations with parents.

Activity Overview

(See *Optional Activity Instructions* for groups of less than 6 or more than 30. These follow the *Trainer Resource: Core Learning Activity Three — Summary of Teaching Points and Answer Guide*.)

Number of participants: 6 to 30

Trainer Resource:

Scenario: Ms. James, Ms. Susan and Jason at Pickup Time (Provide copies for each "actor" participating in the skit.)

Summary of Teaching Points and Answer Guide (for Training Segment #2)

Handout: (CLA3-1) Problem Solving Situations: Opportunities for Building Alliances with Families

Time needed: 2 hours and 30 Minutes (or split into two sessions)

1 Hour for Segment #1

15 Minutes for Break

1 Hour and 15 Minutes for Segment #2

Space: Enough space to perform a skit and set up tables and chairs for writing activities and small group work

CONDUCTING THE ACTIVITY

This learning activity is divided into two segments. Use the Training Notes for each segment to introduce and facilitate workshop activities. Use the following material to introduce the workshop to your staff. The statements in BLUE can be used as a "script" for introducing the activity. Additional notes, instructions or clarifications for the trainer appear in *ITALICS*.

Trainer Notes for Segment #1: Exploring a scenario depicting an interaction between a parent, child and staff member

Before conducting the activity, enlist two staff members to help you act out the scenario. As the trainer, play the role of the parent, Ms. James. Have one staff member play the role of Ms. Susan and another play the role of Jason.

To form alliances with parents as resourceful partners, it is important for us to view each family's circumstances objectively. Sometimes, this can be very challenging. Sometimes it is tempting to make judgments about parents, based on very brief interactions with them, especially when these interactions are unpleasant or frustrating. When our observations do not provide enough information, we need to step back and ask ourselves what else we need to know to connect with parents in a positive way. To demonstrate this, we are going to perform a short skit featuring an interaction between a parent, a child and an after-school program staff member. (Have your fellow actors join you now.) Pretend you are witnessing this scene in our program. As you watch and listen, jot down some notes to help you recall exactly what happens. Also identify questions you think need to be answered before you could decide how to respond effectively to the situation. After we finish the skit, you will use your notes to work with a partner to develop written descriptions of what happened in the skit.

CORE LEARNING ACTIVITY THREE

Ms. James, Ms. Susan and Jason at Pickup Time

The scene: Ms. James runs into the school-age program at 5:30 P.M. She is out of breath, wearing a frown and checking her watch. She looks for her son, Jason. When she doesn't see him, she calls across the room to the closest staff person.

Ms. James: (continuing to check watch) "Ms. Susan, where is Jason? I need to go right now. My car is running in the parking lot."

Ms. Susan: (smiling) "Hi, Ms. James! Jason is in the building area. He has been building a fantastic tower and bridge for over an hour. He's really proud of himself; I'm sure he would like you to see it if you have minute."

Ms. James: (checking watch again) "Well, I don't have time — not even a minute. I had to leave the car motor running because I have our cats in the car and I didn't want them to get chilled. I have to get them to the vet before he closes at 6:00. Please tell Jason to hurry up."

Ms. Susan: (sighing) "OK. Maybe you could plan to stay a few minutes tomorrow when you come to pick up Jason. He and some friends have been learning some magic tricks and they're going to put on a show for the other kids at the end of the day."

Ms. James: (anxiously looking again at her watch) "Really? Well, I don't think I can do that tomorrow. I have to join my husband for a very important dinner with a big client. I'm going to have to get right home so I'll be ready when he stops to pick me up. Maybe some other time — though I don't know when. I have something scheduled every day for the next week; I have some health problems to deal with. My mother is coming for a visit to help out; maybe she can come in and see what Jason is doing."

Jason: (running up to his mom) "Mom, Mom, come and see my tower. It's awesome!"

Ms. James: "I can't Jason. We have to go. I told you this morning to be ready when I got here. Don't you remember?"

Jason: "Yeah, but it'll just take a second."

Ms. James: "I said NO, Jason. Let's go, right now."

Jason: (looking down) "You never have time to see my stuff. Why are you in such a hurry? You don't care about anything I do."

Ms. James: "Don't be rude, Jason. Of course I care about you. That's why Daddy and I pay for you to come here. We know you have a good time!"

Jason: "If you really cared, you'd look at my tower. It's the same every day. You always have something more important to do. I bet you won't have time for my magic show tomorrow."

Ms. James: "No I won't have time, Jason. Maybe Grandma can visit you here next week. She would love to see what you're doing."

Jason: (fists clenched) "I don't want Grandma. I want you or Dad! I'm going to knock my tower down if you won't look at it. (Runs off, knocks down his tower and comes back with tears in his eyes)

Ms. James: "He's just impossible I don't have the time or the patience for his temper tantrums. Jason, we are leaving — NOW."

Jason: (looking at Ms. Susan) "But I didn't clean up my mess."

Ms. James (looking at Susan) "I'm sure Ms. Susan wouldn't mind picking up the blocks for you. She knows I need to go."

Ms. Susan: (helping Jason with his coat). "Sure. Don't worry about it, Jason. Maybe I can help you build another tower. See you tomorrow."

Ms. James and Jason leave the building, frowning and not speaking to each other. Ms. James mumbles to herself, "I just can't handle all this."

DISCUSSION — SEGMENT #1

When the skit is over, use the following material to continue the learning activity.

Before we discuss what happened in this skit, I'd like you to work with a partner and use your notes to develop <u>two written versions</u> of what happened in the skit. For Version One, write down whatever thoughts and attitudes come to mind, including any judgments or emotional statements that occur to you. For Version Two, try to write a description that is objective and nonjudgmental. In Version Two, include any questions that come to mind about what you saw and heard — that is, are there things you don't know about Ms. James's circumstances that might help you understand and respond appropriately to her actions?

Examples of questions might include: "What are the health problems Ms. James referred to?" "Is Ms. James feeling overwhelmed by her health problems?" "Why is Grandma coming to help out?" "How long will Grandma be staying?" "Why has Ms. James scheduled so many activities?" "Is it possible the overscheduling relates to getting a lot of things done before she deals with her health problems?"

After about fifteen minutes, we'll share our different descriptions and how they might affect the relationship between Ms. James and Ms. Susan.

Allow about fifteen minutes for partners to write down their descriptions of the scenario. Then, ask for volunteers to share their descriptions with the group. After several descriptions have been read, conduct a discussion of the scenario, using the following questions as a guide.

Discussion Questions:

- What are some of the differences between Version One and Version Two descriptions? Which versions would be most useful in developing a plan to work effectively with Ms. James? Why?

- Was it difficult to write descriptions that are objective and nonjudgmental? If so, why?

- Why is it important to view interactions with parents objectively? What might happen if school-age staff form quick judgments or focus mainly on subjective impressions of parents?

- Based on interactions in this scenario, what are some of the problems facing Ms. James? What additional information might Ms. Susan need to know in order to build a positive relationship with Ms. James?

- What are some things Ms. Susan could do to provide help and support to Ms. James and Jason?

- What interactions with parents in our program could be handled more effectively if we maintained a nonjudgmental approach toward the parents? What additional information do we need to connect with these parents in a positive way?

Close Training Segment #1 by acknowledging how challenging it can be to remain objective and nonjudgmental. At the same time, emphasize that it is impossible to build alliances with parents if we harbor judgments and resentments. Tell participants that the next segment of the training is designed to help them practice problem-solving techniques that can be helpful in building alliances with parents. Allow a fifteen-minute break before proceeding or schedule another session for conducting Training Segment #2.

DISCUSSION – SEGMENT #2

Use the following information to introduce and conduct the activity.

To build positive relationships and strong alliances with parents in our program, we often need to work together to reach out to parents who may need our support and help as they work through challenges and difficulties. In this learning activity, we are going to explore a variety of problem situations that parents in out-of-school programs might experience and develop strategies for building relationships with the families in each situation.

Distribute the handout: **Problem-Solving Situations: Opportunities for Building Alliances with Families Handout (CLA-3-1)**. *(This handout includes problem situations involving parents from a variety of backgrounds — focus on those situations that might be similar to those of parents in your own program. Consider supplementing the handout with "home grown" situations that are directly related to the circumstances of parents in your program.) The handout begins on the next page. Continue introducing the activity as follows.*

We will work in small groups of three or four participants to examine the situations and brainstorm solutions for providing assistance and support to the families described in each situation. I'll assign two or three situations to each group. You will notice that each situation provides <u>objective, nonjudgmental</u> background information about the families. As we discussed earlier, effective plans for building alliances with parents always begin with taking an objective, nonjudgmental look at the families' circumstances and needs. In addition, effective problem-solving involves using a systematic step-by-step approach. Before we break into groups for this activity, let's look at the Problem-Solving Tips listed at the beginning of the handout.

Review the Problem-Solving Tips and Instructions on the handout before proceeding. Emphasize that PROBLEMS are really OPPORTUNITIES to make improvements and/or needed changes. Reconvene the group after thirty minutes and facilitate a discussion using the **Summary of Teaching Points and Answer Guide** *that follow the* **Problem-Solving Situations** *handout as a resource.*

CORE LEARNING ACTIVITY THREE

Problem-Solving Situations:
Opportunities for Building
Alliances with Parents

INSTRUCTIONS

Work in small groups to explore strategies for working through the problems and challenges in the situations assigned to your group. Appoint one person to lead your group and another to take notes. You will have about 30 minutes for small group discussion. Designate one group member to share your ideas with the larger group.

Problem-Solving Tips:

As you discuss each situation, use a problem-solving approach to the questions posed. The following step-by-step approach should be helpful as you explore each situation:

- Stop and identify the possible or probable causes of the problems described in each situation assigned to your group. Ask: What additional information would be helpful to know?

- Brainstorm a list of possible strategies for assisting each family.

- Discuss the pros and cons of each possible strategy.

- Choose the strategies you think would be most effective in providing help and support to the families.

- Discuss how you could follow up to learn if your problem-solving strategies were effective.

Situation One

Several families in your program live in a low-income neighborhood where most children are on their own when school is out. As a result of your community outreach efforts, these families decided to enroll their children in your program instead of leaving them in self-care. However, they are skeptical and have reservations about your program. They are not really sure that supervised care is necessary. They also wonder whether it is a good idea to trust their children to strangers who may not understand their values, family traditions and attitudes about child rearing. A number of the parents who have concerns do not know how to read. Some speak languages other than English.

Questions:

- What specifically can you do to gain the confidence of these parents and help them feel comfortable with the program?

- What could you do to get them involved in some aspect of the program?

Situation Two

A large number of children in your program come from single-parent homes. Knowing this, you have tried to be supportive and understanding of the problems that face these families. One of these single parents has recently gone through a traumatic divorce and has been trying to complete her college education while holding down a full-time job. As a result, she has several night classes and has no one to pick up her child from the program at the end of the day. She found out she lives in your neighborhood and asks you to give her child a ride home every day (even though it is against the program's policy for staff to transport children in their cars). She also asks you to baby-sit in the evenings and on weekends.

Questions:

- How would you start a conversation to help her with her concerns?

- What can you do to help this parent handle her need for transportation and child-care services?

Situation Three

One of the fifth grade boys in your program is always swearing and calling people names; sometimes he hits other kids without any provocation. Most of the time he wears a scowl. He often comes to the program wearing clothing that is either dirty or torn. When you mention his behavior to his grandmother who picks him up every day, she tells you that you just have to be firm with him. "He's always up to no good ever since his dad left — you just have to show him who is boss. If he doesn't do what you say, tell him he can't have a snack or don't let him play basketball. That's what we do at home. Nothing else seems to work."

Questions:

- What would you say in response to the grandmother's suggestions?

- What can you do to build a relationship with this family to be helpful to the child?

Situation Four

The father of eight-year-old Jamie is a truck driver and is frequently out of town for days and sometimes weeks at a time. Although Jamie's mother works hard to stay informed about program activities and her son's experiences there, Jamie often talks about how much he misses his father when he's away.

Questions:

- How would you approach talking about this problem with Jamie's mother and/or father?

- What are some ways you could help Jamie's father be more connected to Jamie's life in the program?

- How would you help Jamie's father if he had a different occupation that required frequent or lengthy travel? Examples: An airline pilot? A regional sales representative for a shoe company? A military person on temporary duty in another country? A newspaper or television reporter? A member of a band or orchestra?

Situation Five

Many of the children in your program come from well-educated, upper-middle income families: college professors, lawyers, doctors and corporate executives. Even though these parents are very busy, they say they are extremely interested in and anxious about what's happening at the center when they aren't there. They have constant questions and concerns about what their children do in the program and how their children are growing and developing. Some of these parents want their children to be exposed to many different types of enrichment activities after school. Others are very concerned that their children finish their homework while they're at the program.

Questions:

- What can you do to ensure that these parents understand what's going on in your program, have confidence in you, support your efforts and get involved in positive ways?

- What can you do to be responsive to the parents who want their children to participate in enrichment activities as well as the parents who want their children to get their homework done?

- How could you give a family-friendly response to the following comments or questions from parents?

  - "When I arrive at 5:30, I want Laura ready to go. I have to pick up her sister at a day-care center across town by 6 o'clock and if I'm not on time, they fine me $5 for every 5 minutes I'm late. So, I can't afford to wait around for Laura, no matter what she's doing."

  - "Danny really wants to learn how to play the guitar, but the only teacher I can find just has openings right after school. I don't get off until 5:00, so there's no way for me to get him there in time. Couldn't you arrange to have some special lessons offered here at the center?"

  - "Will you please see to it that Greg does his homework here at the program? He's so tired after supper, I have a lot of trouble getting him to do his homework in the evening and we always end up in an argument."

  - "Arielle says she usually spends every afternoon playing outside with her friend Sasha. I don't want to pay high fees just for her to run around outside. Aren't there other activities she could do where she could be learning something?"

  - "Whenever I ask Carlos what he did at the program, he says 'Not much.' Is that really true? I'm really worried he is wasting his time here."

Situation Six

Several of the children in your program come from young two-parent families where both parents work and are struggling to make ends meet. The mother in one of these families is a graphic artist; the father is a sales representative for a sporting-goods company. Although they work very hard at being successful, they always seem to be in a hurry. Their children sometimes complain that they have to leave home in the morning before they have finished breakfast. And because the parents are frequently late at pickup time, the children often worry that something may have happened to them. Because these parents usually rush in and out at pick-up time, you rarely have a chance to talk with them.

Questions:

- What would you say to begin a discussion of the problem with these parents?

- What could you do to help these parents cope with some of the pressures they are experiencing?

- What strategies could you use to communicate effectively and build an alliance with these parents?

Situation Seven

Parents of some of the older children in your program are upset because their children aren't able to participate in community sports leagues (soccer and baseball). The practices start at 6:00 PM on weekdays and these parents aren't available to transport their children from your program to practice until 6:30. Both soccer and baseball leagues hold their practices at community fields that are located about a mile from your site. Parents are especially concerned because their children's school is devoting less and less time to physical activity during the school day. They think their children really need regular exercise and time to play physical games. Their children frequently talk about how disappointed they are about not playing on community teams.

Questions:

- What could your program do to help these parents and their children get involved with community sports leagues?

- If participation with leagues cannot be arranged, what other options could be explored to involve these children in team sports after school?

Situation Eight

Several parents in your program have complained about the way some of the girls in the program dress. They think that very short mini-skirts are provocative and that girls should "keep their middles covered up." They are especially concerned that some of the girls roll down their sweat pants way below their belly buttons. They want the program to do something about it.

Questions:

- What could staff do to ensure that children dress appropriately at the program?

- How could children be involved in solving the problem?

- How could parents be involved in a positive way to address this issue?

Situation Nine

Ned, a fourth-grader in your program, is from a family where recently divorced parents are sharing custody. The custody agreement provides that Ned lives with each parent a specified number of days a week. As a result, Dad picks up Ned at the program on some nights, and Mom picks up on other nights. Ned alternates living with Mom or Dad every other weekend. You are beginning to notice that Dad often doesn't share information with Mom. When Dad picked up Ned on Tuesday, you gave him a weekly memo about program events, a field trip permission form and notice of a field trip fee. He said, "Thanks, I'll take care of it." The form and fee were to be returned by Friday, Mom's pick-up day. When you asked Mom about this on Friday, she didn't know anything about it. She shook her head and said, "He's driving me crazy; he never tells me anything! I don't know what to do."

Questions:

- What could staff do to improve communication between this family and the program?

- What could staff do to support Ned as he moves between two homes?

Situation Ten

Several parents of older children in your program requested a meeting to talk to you about their concerns that some of the kids in the program may be part of a local gang. They told you that the kids that concern them always seem to be wearing colors associated with the gang. They've noticed that these kids sometimes have certain symbols drawn on their faces and hands. They've also noticed that someone has been drawing these same symbols on some of the program furniture and on the wall near a bulletin board. They're afraid their kids might get involved with a gang. They tell you they enrolled their kids in your program to keep them safe and now it looks like the dangers of the street have come to the program.

Questions:

- How can you find out if the parents' concerns are warranted?

- What are some ways you can work with parents in your program to address potential gang problems?

Situation Eleven

Your program provides excellent after-school services for elementary-school children. A number of children who have been in your program for five years will move on to middle-school next year. Their parents recently discovered there is no community after-school program for middle-school kids. Some of these parents think their kids will be fine on their own after school. But others are concerned that their children won't have the skills or maturity to spend every day alone after school. They ask you: "Why doesn't your program serve middle-school kids, too? They're still kids and they need supervision! Why do you abandon them, just when they could really get in trouble?"

Questions:

- What suggestions and advice could you offer these parents?

- What could your current program do to help address the concerns of these parents?

Summary of Teaching Points and Answer Guide

INSTRUCTIONS

After 30 minutes of small group work, use this *Summary of Teaching Points and Answer Guide* to facilitate sharing of problem-solving ideas for building alliances with parents in the situations.

Summary of Teaching Points for This Activity

- It is important for school-age staff to reserve judgment and make objective observations of parents in order to build positive relationships.

- It is important for school-age staff to ask themselves what they need to know about families' situations and experiences in order to provide appropriate help and support.

- Strong alliances with parents as resourceful partners are built by accepting parents, considering their needs and concerns, and following through by working together with parents to come up with strategies that will address their needs and concerns.

- School-age programs often can use parents' problems and concerns as opportunities for building alliances with parents.

- It is important for school-age staff to develop and use effective communication skills and step-by-step problem-solving skills when building relationships and alliances with parents.

ANSWER GUIDE FOR THIS ACTIVITY

There are many possible ways to address the situations provided for this activity. Ideas for working through each situation begin below. Often, the possible solutions could be used in combinations. There is usually not one single solution to the problems presented. Refer to the following examples of solutions during large group discussion as appropriate.

Situation One

- Invite parents to visit the program to observe or share family traditions and customs.

- Purchase program materials, equipment and supplies that reflect the cultural backgrounds of the children enrolled.

- Invite bilingual parents to help write the program newsletter and have it printed in additional languages.

- Recruit staff or volunteers who can speak to the parents in their primary language(s).

- Research the availability of volunteers to help translate program materials (for example, school language teachers or specialists).

Situation Two

Talk with the parent about some of the potential difficulties that might arise if you become the special baby sitter for one child in the program. Then:

- Help the parent locate community organizations and agencies that could provide assistance.

- Help the parent identify others in the neighborhood who might be interested in baby-sitting.

- Help the parent network with other parents in the program that might be interested in exchanging baby-sitting services.

- Share the parent's problem with your supervisor to determine whether there might be other ways the program could help this parent and others with similar problems.

Situation Three

- Encourage the grandmother to share more information about the difficulties the child is experiencing at home. Acknowledge these difficulties.

- Share information about the program's philosophy, discipline policies and procedures, making it clear that staff at the center may not withhold food or physical activity as punishment. Invite the grandmother to help you come up with other ways to help the child gain self-control.

- Express your genuine concern(s) about the child's hygiene and behavior. Give objective examples; avoid making judgmental comments. (For example, instead of "He always looks like a slob," say "Even though his pants are streaked with dirt and spots of grease, he often wears them all week long; his shirts are often missing several buttons.")

- Offer to provide the grandmother with information about community-resource people who might be able to provide assistance to the family.

Situation Four

- Post a map at the program and help the child track his father's itinerary.

- Invite the father to send postcards directly to his son at the program.

- Invite the family to send in pictures the child can use to make a family poster or album to keep at the program.

- Invite the father to visit the program and talk about what it is like to be a truck driver, what types of things he hauls, where he eats and sleeps while on the road. If possible, invite him to bring his truck and give the kids a truck tour.

- Invite the father to record some of the child's favorite stories, jokes or songs on cassette tapes and make the tapes available to the child when the father is away on trips.

Situation Five

- Provide parents with brochures, handbooks, regular newsletters and memos about the program — its philosophy, program of activities, policies and procedures.

- Post pictures of staff members along with short biographies about their education, experience, interests, talents and skills on the parent bulletin board. Highlight the professional background of staff in the parent newsletter.

- Encourage parents to visit the program at any time and on special occasions.

- Work with the children to create a cozy, inviting, attractive homework area. Give the homework center a clubhouse atmosphere and a catchy name (for example, "Homework Haven") so that children will want to go there to complete their homework.

- Make a video of program activities and encourage parents to check it out for weekend viewing with their children.

Situation Six

- Write brief notes to the parents, highlighting their children's activities at the program.

- Ask the parents for a convenient time when you could call or visit with them briefly about their children's experiences. In the conversation, communicate your observation that the parents seem pressured and rushed for time. Acknowledge the difficulties of balancing work and family demand. Ask if there are ways the program might help ease the pressure — for example, consider organizing a breakfast club for children who may not have enough time to eat at home in the morning.

- Conduct a brief survey to determine whether parents would like to receive information or participate in workshops or seminars that offer help in balancing work and family pressures.

- Recognize that parents who don't have time to contribute to the program may be willing to get involved in other ways that might enhance the program. In this case, parents might contribute surplus sporting-goods equipment, excess paper or other graphics supplies).

Situation Seven

- Facilitate a meeting between representatives of community soccer and baseball leagues, parents of children in your program who want to play in those leagues and program staff. At the meeting, talk about possible solutions to the problem. (For example, can transportation be arranged from the program to the practices? Can any teams hold their practices at your program site?)

- Plan ongoing team sports in your program. Explore ways to link sports activities at your program with those offered in other after-school programs. (For example, can kids who play on teams in your program schedule games with kids who play on teams at a nearby after-school program?)

- Recruit community volunteers to lead team sports activities and teach sports skills to children and youth in your program. (For example, can team members and/or coaches of local high school or college teams or amateur sports leagues donate time to lead sports activities for kids in your program once a week?)

- Be an advocate who supports sports activities after school for all children. Speak up, lead from within your organization and encourage decision makers to provide funding for team sports in your program.

Situation Eight

- Convene a meeting with parents to discuss their concerns about dress — what they think is appropriate and inappropriate. Encourage parents to talk with their children about dressing appropriately and monitor what their children are wearing when they leave home. Share parents' concerns from the meeting with other parents in the program through a newsletter or memo. Contact individual parents privately about a child's inappropriate dress, if needed.

- If the school(s) that children attend have a dress code, find out about the details. If appropriate, require children to follow the school dress code in your program as well. Communicate this decision to parents and children in the program through policy handbooks, newsletters, posters, etc.

- Get kids involved in monitoring their own dress behavior. Help them create kid-generated guidelines that respect parents' concerns and reflect appropriate dress for kids in the program. Talk about what we communicate by the way we dress. Also talk about dress as an expression of self-respect and respect for others.

- Start a fashion club to help kids explore creative, fun ways to dress that allow self-expression, but also exhibit self-respect and respect for others.

- Ensure that program staff are positive role models for appropriate dress.

Situation Nine

- Request a conference with both parents to talk about how you can work together to keep communication running smoothly.

- Create two parent mail boxes in the program for Ned's parents — one for Mom and one for Dad; make duplicates of all memos and communications to parents and be sure both parents get all of them.

- Use e-mail to communicate time-sensitive information and due dates for returning permission slips, etc. Copy both parents on every e-mail.

- Post reminders of due dates, special program closings and any program changes prominently on the parent bulletin board. Urge Ned's parents to check the board regularly to help them stay up to date.

- Create a special folder for Ned to take between home and the program that includes samples of his work, photos of him at play, etc. Have Ned keep all items in the folder for one week so that both parents will have an opportunity to see what he's been up to. Work with Ned to change the folder when a new week begins.

Situation Ten

- Conduct observations of children in your program and of the program environment to assess the extent to which parents' concerns about gangs may be warranted. Share your observations with colleagues and your supervisor.

- Contact the schools and the local police department to learn what they know about possible gang-related activity in your community.

- Arrange a meeting where school, police representatives, program and other community representatives can share concerns and/or allay fears about gang-related activities with parents in your program.

- Work with parents and colleagues to develop a plan for addressing concerns about gangs in your program. Request the help of police, schools, youth agencies and other community-resource people to develop a gang-prevention program or campaign that includes workshops for parents and strategies and activities for helping kids resist participation in gang-related activities.

Situation Eleven

- Arrange a meeting for these parents to express their concerns about the need for after-school services for middle-school children.

- Arrange a meeting with parents and community representatives who could work together to conduct a needs survey and create a plan for initiating services for middle-school children.

- Investigate ways that your own program could provide services for these children. For example: Could you develop a special component of your program for older children and arrange daily transportation for these children to return to your site from middle school? (For example, could you develop a counselor-in-training program or a mentoring program where children who are "graduating" from your program could stay on in the program in the role of helper? Could you offer special skill clubs, sports clubs, craft clubs, homework clubs or other activities aimed at early adolescents?)

Optional Activity Instructions

If time is limited and/or there are more than 30 participants, assign only one situation to each small group, rather than having each small group discuss two or three situations. This will allow you to reduce the amount of time allotted for small group discussion so that you will have enough time to share ideas from each group during the large group discussion.

For groups smaller than six, keep the group together to discuss the situations, rather than dividing into groups.

Prepare for the Next Session

At the end of **Core Learning Activity Three***, distribute a handout for* **Core Learning Activity Four: Exploring Parent Roles***. Ask staff to read it before the next session. See* **Core Learning Activity Four** *to locate the handout and for directions for introducing the reading assignment.*

Core Learning Activity Four

Exploring Parent Roles

Preliminary Notes

The task of being a parent parallels children's growth and development. Just as children grow and change as they develop, noted researcher Ellen Galinsky asserts that parents grow and change as they move from one stage of parenthood to the next. Galinsky conducted extensive interviews with 228 parents (of 396 children) who had diverse experiences in parenthood — married, divorced, widowed, step, foster, adoptive and guardian mothers and fathers. She talked with teenage parents and older parents, parents expecting their first child and those with large families. The children of these families included those who were gifted and those who possessed challenging special needs. The parents included a wide range of economic, ethnic, racial, geographic and religious backgrounds. Galinsky analyzed these interviews and presented her conclusions in the book *The Six Stages of Parenthood*.

According to Galinsky's findings, the experience of parenthood is complex and diverse. However, within the diversity, Galinsky was able to identify common threads and similar ways that people perceived their experiences as parents. Galinsky traces six distinct stages in the life of a parent in relation to their growing child. By taking a look at these different stages, those who work with children and youth in out-of-school programs can gain some insight about parental needs and concerns.

A summary of Galinsky's six stages is presented in **Core Learning Activity Four** handout ***The Six Stages of Parenthood*** that begins on page 56. More detail is provided for *Stage Four: Interpretive* and *Stage Five: Interdependent*, because these stages describe the parental tasks and concerns of parents of elementary- and middle-school children, the age group commonly served by school-age programs. The other stages are briefly summarized to provide a broad overview of the tasks of parenthood over the life of each child. It is important to remember that parents of school-age children may be parenting children at other stages as well; it can be quite a challenge for parents to move in and out of different stages during the course of a day!

Activity Overview

Number of Participants: Any number

Handouts:

CLA4-1 The Six Stages of Parenthood

CLA4-2 Small Group Exercise: Discussion Questions

Time Needed: 30 minutes in advance of the session; 1 hour during the session

Space: Any area suitable for large and small group discussions among participants

CONDUCTING THE ACTIVITY

*Distribute the handout **The Six Stages of Parenthood** at the end of **Learning Activity Three**. The handout appears on the next page. Ask staff to read the handout before the next session. Use the **Preliminary Notes** for this activity to introduce the handout.*

At the next session, begin by providing a brief overview and facilitate a discussion of the Six Stages of Parenthood, following these steps:

- *Use the handout as a resource for providing the overview.*

- *Share anecdotes from your own life experience to bring each stage of parenthood to life.*

- *Invite staff to share their life experiences with each stage (for example, their own experiences as a parent if they are parents, their perceptions of their own parents at each stage, experiences they have observed in parents of children who are close to them).*

- *Encourage staff to ask questions and share comments about each stage.*

After the overview and discussion, divide staff into groups of four to six participants. Distribute the handout **Small Group Exercise: Discussion Questions.** Use the following material to introduce the workshop to your staff. The statements in BLUE can be used as a "script" for introducing the activity. Additional notes, instructions or clarifications for the trainer appear in *ITALICS*.

Parents in our program are moving through the *Interpretive Stage* of parenthood in relation to their school-age children between the ages of 5 and 12.

(Note: The handout Small Group Exercise: Discussion Questions includes questions related to the *Interpretive Stage* and the *Interdependent Stage*. If your program serves children between the ages of 13 and 14, focus on the *Interdependent Stage* of parenthood for this activity. If you serve children from 5 to 14, have some groups discuss the questions related to the *Interpretive Stage* and others discuss the questions related to the Interdependent Stage).

> For this activity we will work in small groups to identify the needs of our parents and explore ways we can support them. Refer to the discussion questions assigned to your group as you share your ideas. Appoint a leader to facilitate your small group discussion. You will have about 20 minutes to work together in your group. Then we'll come back together to share and compare our ideas.

Locate the handout Small Group Exercise: Discussion Questions immediately after the handout **The Six Stages of Parenthood.**

After 20 minutes, reconvene the larger group and facilitate a group discussion where small groups share their ideas.

CORE LEARNING ACTIVITY FOUR

The Six Stages of Parenthood*

STAGE ONE: IMAGE-MAKING

According to researcher Ellen Galinsky, parents begin to shape their role as parents even before the child arrives on the scene. They begin to create pictures in their minds of what lies ahead as they form images of birth and parenthood. Galinsky stresses that this imagining of what lies ahead is a lifelong process. As parents go through each stage of parenthood, they continue to work with these images. Growth occurs at points when parents modify an image to be more consistent with reality or modify their own behavior to reach toward an image. While some parents resist or turn away from growth, Galinsky's interviews revealed that people do change; that parenthood is itself a transforming experience.

STAGE TWO: NURTURING

This stage goes from birth until the child begins to say "No," somewhere around eighteen months to two years. In this stage, parents compare their images of birth, of their child and of themselves as parents with their actual experience. Whether there is a substantial discrepancy between the imagined and actual child, it is by getting to know the child that the parents can resolve these differences — by holding, touching, caring for the baby. A process of bonding takes place. They become attached to the baby. As parents face feelings of attachment, they work through a variety of questions and issues. They face questions about their priorities, about how much time they should give to the baby and how much time to devote to other aspects of life.

STAGE THREE: AUTHORITY

This stage goes approximately from the child's second to the child's fourth or fifth year. In this stage, Galinsky says, parents face the task of deciding what kind of authority to be, how rules are set, what the rules are, when they are enforced and what happens when they are broken. The theme of control versus lack of control reaches a peak and predominates in the *Authority Stage*. In this stage, parents are sure of their identity as parents and have an attachment to the child. Now they face the major task of accepting their authority over the child and begin to understand that the child is not really an extension of them. Most parents approach parenthood with expectations about the kind of disciplinarian they are going to be. They may form images about not getting angry, always being capable of unconditional love or being a different kind of disciplinarian than their parents were. They may also have images about children — that children are always nice or that children will stay the same from one year to the next. Images that work can be kept; others must be revised in order for the parent and child to grow harmoniously. Problems in the parent/child relationship are inevitable. The question during the *Authority Stage* becomes how to resolve the problems that occur — for

---

* Excerpted and adapted with permission from Ellen Galinsky, *The Six Stages of Parenthood*. Reading, MA: Perseus Books. 1987.

parents it means facing the challenge of becoming an authority and developing the skills to play the authority role appropriately.

STAGE FOUR: INTERPRETIVE

Generally, this stage encompasses the elementary-school years. It begins in the child's preschool years and ends with the approach of adolescence. The child's entrance into kindergarten or first grade usually prompts parents to review their images of parenthood, to ask themselves how realistic they've been. By evaluating the past, they prepare themselves for changes to come. Through self-evaluations, parents can become more realistic about themselves and about their children. The task at this stage is interpreting. Although parents recognize they are not the only ones who influence their child, they are concerned with how they are interpreting themselves to their children as well as how they are interpreting and developing their children's self-concepts. They also are figuring out how they want to interpret reality, how to answer their children's questions and what types of knowledge, skills and values to promote. A part of this process for parents involves evaluating their children. These evaluations are based on the images they have held on to and the comparisons to siblings or classmates or neighborhood children. These evaluations must be reconciled with the child's self-concept and with the judgments that others (for example, teachers, child-care staff) make about the child. During this stage, the child also begins to create images of what a parent should be like and some of his images are in conflict with the images he has of his parent(s). Defining the increasing separateness of their own and their child's identity while holding onto the connectedness continues to be a task in the *Interpretive Stage*. The older the child gets, the more the parent realizes that "My child is not me."

The tasks in the *Interpretive Stage* require parents to decide how they will interpret their children's existence to them. Sometimes parents fall into these decisions; other times the decisions are chosen. An overview of the parental decisions to be made in the *Interpretive Stage*:

- Deciding what kind of life they want to and can afford to provide. Questions of giving and getting are often focused on material things. Parents have to decide when to say "yes" and when to say "no" to children's requests for clothes, toys, sporting equipment, etc.

- Deciding how to interpret facts, skills and experiences to their children (for example, bad dreams, a bank robbery down the street, a teacher the child thinks is not fair, a neighbor who is not kind to his pets, the meaning of words such as "incest" or "rape" in response to the child's questions). In addition to interpreting or telling, parents during this stage are listening.

- Deciding how they want their children to behave (manners, household chores, etc.).

- Deciding how involved to be in the children's lives, at home and away from home. This decision relates not only to the child, but to how much time parents need for themselves as individuals, for their work, for each other.

- Deciding when and how much to step in, to do things with one's children. Deciding when to let go, to encourage the children to do things independently.

- Deciding how involved to become with the other significant people, children and adults, in their own children's lives (teachers, counselors, child-care staff, social workers, parents of the child's friends, etc.)

- Deciding how to define the changing relationship between parent and child. For example, the physical relationship between parent and child is changing. How much do parents and children hug, hold, cuddle and kiss as the child continues to grow and develop?

As they wrestle with all these decisions, Galinsky emphasizes that parents in the *Interpretive Stage* must involve themselves in the task of redefining the *Authority* relationship. They must respond to children's concepts of fairness as their children master new reasoning skills. In families with several children, parents have the task of dealing with conflict between their children. As they deal with these issues, many parents experience a feeling of slipping in and out of control. They have to continue to figure out how they are going to handle family spats, competitions, accusations and put-downs.

Throughout the *Interpretive Stage*, parents respond to children's easy and not-so-easy questions and concerns. This causes parents to review what they think, believe and value. It causes them to pull together their own beliefs so they can translate them to their children. This is a demanding, challenging process for all parents in this stage.

STAGE FIVE: INTERDEPENDENT

This stage spans the child's teenage years. The issues that predominated in the *Authority Stage* rise back into prominence. This stage begins when parents become aware of what often seem to be unexpected, sometimes even shocking changes in the child — changes in clothing, behavior toward the opposite sex, language, hairstyle, physical growth, etc. Because the changes are often dramatic, the actual entry into this stage can abruptly challenge images about who the child is. Galinsky emphasizes that today's parents field many problems that they feel inexperienced in handling. The dangers today are bigger, and yet parents' power is diminishing. With this in mind, there are two important facets parents must concentrate on as they redefine the authority relationship: communicating with teenagers; and setting limits and giving guidance

To handle these issues effectively, parents must know themselves — their own standards and expectations and they must know their teenager — how much guidance he or she needs. During the *Interdependent Stage*, the parent must also accept that the teenager's major task is developing a separate identity. Separation is a gradual process. Through this stage, the parent/child relationship is redefined. The new relationship involves swinging between distance and closeness, separateness and connectedness. The major task of this stage is redefining the parent/child relationship. Some of the related sub-tasks for parents in the *Interdependent Stage*:

- Re-examining their images of who the child is and who the child is becoming. Redefining images that aren't workable.

- Learning about the stages of adolescence as a tool for increasing understanding of their children.

- Shoring up old ways of communicating and developing new ways to facilitate talking together.

- Responding to what teenagers say and do and what they don't say and do by setting limits and giving guidance.

- Clarifying their own standards and expectations for their teenager to resolve important questions such as:

  - Who makes decisions about what?

  - How will decisions be enforced?

  - What does the future hold for the teenager — finishing high school, going to college, going to work?

  - Where is the teenager allowed to go? With whom? By what method of transportation?

  - What about smoking, drinking, drugs and sex?

  - How will money issues be handled and resolved?

- Changing as the teenager changes and avoiding battles of wills.

- Accepting the teenager's identity, including sexual roles, and dealing with feelings of affinity and dissimilarity to their child.

- Evaluating their roles as parents and dealing with the evaluations their children are making of them.

- Creating new bonds with an almost-grown child.

Parents are inevitably changed as they work on these tasks and move through the *Interdependent Stage* with their teenager.

STAGE SIX: DEPARTURE

The time when the child leaves home is characterized by evaluations. Parents evaluate whether they have achieved the parent/grown-child relationship they wanted as well as taking stock of their overall success and failures. They form images about what the future will bring: How far away their child might go and how often they will be together. Often, the *Departure Stage* spans a long period of time. During the *Departure Stage*, parents search for new ways to say they are still a family by creating new rituals, habits and traditions. In the *Departure Stage* parents have the task of loosening their control even more. It involves a complex set of tasks: caring, being available, helping without controlling, accepting the grown child's separate identity. In accepting this separate identity, parents learn that to accept separateness implies the beginning of a new connection.

CORE LEARNING ACTIVITY FOUR

Small Group Exercise: Discussion Questions

INSTRUCTIONS

Focus on the stage of parenthood that parallels the ages of children and youth in your program. If you serve children between the ages of 5 and 12, focus on questions related to the *Interpretive Stage*. If you serve children between the ages of 13 and 14, focus on questions related to the *Interdependent Stage*. Discuss each of the questions assigned to your small group. Appoint a group leader and someone to take notes. Throughout your discussions, refer to the handout *The Six Stages of Parenthood* as needed. Have your group leader summarize your consensus on each question in preparation for sharing your ideas with the larger group.

Questions Related to the Interpretive Stage:

1. What signs do you see that parents may be struggling with deciding when to say "yes" and when to say "no" to their children's requests for material things? What could you do to help these parents deal with these issues?

2. What signs do you see that parents may be having difficulty interpreting life events and experiences to their children (for example, catastrophic news events, tragedies in the community, political controversies, etc.)? How could you provide support to help these parents?

3. What signs do you see that parents may be struggling with setting and maintaining standards for their children's behavior in relation to exhibiting good manners, showing respect, following through on responsibilities, etc.? What could you do to help these parents develop suitable techniques for guiding behavior?

4. What signs do you see that parents are struggling with how to relate to their children's growing need for independence? How could you help these parents find the right balance as they help their children move toward independence?

5. What signs do you see that parents may be having difficulty figuring out the best way(s) to get involved in their children's lives? (For example, finding time to attend meetings, volunteering, participating on committees or boards; interacting with children's teachers, coaches, child-care providers, etc.) How could you help these parents develop a workable approach to getting involved?

6. What signs do you see that parents are working on defining the changing relationship between themselves and their children? What support could you offer to parents who are trying to become comfortable with this changing relationship?

Questions Related to the Interdependent Stage:

1. What signs do you see that parents are having difficulty developing new, effective ways of talking with their teenagers and sharing ideas? What could you do to help parents develop effective ways of communicating with their teenage children?

2. What signs do you see that parents are struggling with setting limits, giving guidance and avoiding power struggles with their changing teenagers? How could you help parents develop more effective ways to guide their children's behavior?

3. What signs do you see that parents are confused or unsure about the stages of adolescence and/or don't understand the changes that children are experiencing? What resources or programs could you offer to help parents learn more about the stages of adolescence?

4. What signs do you see that parents are facing challenges related to clarifying their own standards and expectations in order to resolve important questions and make decisions with their teenagers? How could you provide help to parents who are finding it difficult to clarify their standards and expectations and strike an appropriate balance of decision-making with their teenagers?

5. What signs do you see that parents are either concerned about or totally unaware of their children's involvement with smoking, drinking, drugs and/or sex? What resources and support could you provide to help parents communicate with their teenagers about these issues?

6. What signs do you see that some parents and children are actively engaged in evaluating each other as parents and as teenagers? How can you help parents and teenagers look at each other in positive ways, regardless of whether their personalities are very similar or very different? How can you help parents and teenagers form new bonds as the children move toward adulthood?

CORE LEARNING ACTIVITY FIVE

What Parents Want and Need From School-Age Programs

PRELIMINARY NOTES

Core Learning Activity Four focused on helping staff understand how the stages of parenthood are directly related to the developmental stages that their children are experiencing. Staff explored the results of research on the *Six Stages of Parenthood* and discussed how these stages are apparent in parents in their programs. They also generated ideas for providing help, support and resources to parents in relation to some of the developmental tasks associated with each stage of parenthood.

Core Learning Activity Five builds on the ideas explored in the last session. It focuses on helping staff understand how the wants and needs of parents are connected to the stages of parenthood that parents are experiencing. This activity is presented in three Training Segments.

Activity Overview

Number of participants: Any number

Trainer resources:
Selected Assessment Tools from Section Two — Optional
1 pencil and sheet of blank paper per group, chart paper and marker (Training Segment Three)

Handouts:
What Do Parents Really Want? (Training Segment One)

Sample List of What Parents Want from School-Age Programs (Training Segment Two)

Time needed: 2 hours and 30 minutes
60 minutes for skit and follow-up discussion
10 minutes for break
60 minutes for identifying parent wants
20 minutes for family friendly game

Space: An area that allows space for performing a skit and for setting up tables and chairs for small group work

CONDUCTING THE ACTIVITY

This **Learning Activity** is divided into three segments. Use the Trainer Notes for each segment to facilitate workshop activities. Use the following material to introduce the workshop to your staff. The statements in BLUE can be used as a "script" for introducing the activity. Additional notes, instructions or clarifications for the trainer appear in *ITALICS*.

Trainer Notes for Segment #1: Skit and Discussion:

What Do Parents Really Want?

In Segment #1, staff observe a skit that stages a conversation among three parents outside a school-age program and then discuss a series of follow-up questions. Before the session begins, ask two staff to assist you in acting out the skit that appears in the handout: *What Do Parents Really Want?* Following the skit, conduct an open-ended large group discussion, allowing staff maximum freedom to add comments, ask questions and give suggestions for improving parent relationships. In addition to the materials provided for this session, refer to the ideas from previous workshops as a resource for guiding discussion. Tools and tip sheets from **Section Two** and **Section Three** of this book may also be useful. Use the following material to introduce the skit.

> I've invited several of your colleagues to help me act out a scenario involving three parents who are having a conversation outside a school-age program. These parents encounter each other in the parking lot before entering the building to pick up their children. As you watch the skit, keep in mind the Interpretive and Interdependent Stages. Try to spot evidence that these parents are grappling with some of the tasks involved in these stages. After the skit, we'll have a group discussion of the needs and wants of these parents and how they relate to the stages of parenthood we've been exploring.

Perform the skit now.

Following the presentation of the skit, distribute the handout: *What Do Parents Really Want?* found on the next page. Refer participants to the questions at the end of the handout. Facilitate a group discussion, using the questions on the handout as a guide. Add your own questions as well as questions from participants as appropriate. Read the following to start the discussion:

> It is clear that the parents in this scene have some common concerns as well as some differences of opinion about what they want from their school-age program. In reaching out to parents, it is important to recognize that parental needs, interests and concerns vary from person to person and may be influenced by family, cultural background and traditions, economic concerns, stresses and pressures in the workplace, values and beliefs about parenthood, educational background, their child's temperament and behavioral style, and many other factors. As you discuss the questions on the handout, keep in mind the differences among parents as well as what they have in common.

CORE LEARNING ACTIVITY FIVE

What Do Parents *Really* Want?

The scene: The following conversation takes place between three parents of school-age children in the parking lot outside a school-age child-care program at pickup time.

Beth: "Hey, Rosa, how are you doing? I haven't seen you for awhile and when I do, you're always in a rush! Is everything OK?"

Rosa: "Good to see you, Beth. I'm fine, I guess. But I'm exhausted. I never seem to have time to relax. Every night, I rush in here after work, rush home to get dinner, and then rush back out again to get Mark to soccer practice. Then I help Lisha with her homework and rush back out again to pick up Mark. Actually, this is the first night I haven't had to hurry in a long time; soccer practice was canceled! So, I thought I'd go in and see what Lisha has been up to. Usually, I have to hurry her out of here, and it's a pretty tense scene. Frankly, I think the staff thinks I don't care about what Lisha does here; I can feel the dirty looks as I try to get her packed up as fast as I can. But it's not true; I have to be on time for Mark or he'll get in trouble with his soccer coach. I really don't want my kids to miss out on anything! But sometimes it's overwhelming!"

Beth: "I'll walk in with you. I always try to stay for a few minutes, just to see what Katie has been up to. She doesn't like to talk about what she does all afternoon. When I ask, she gives me the feeling I'm invading her privacy. But I like to see how the staff treat her; I want her to feel like they care about her. By the way, have you met Jim? He just enrolled his son, Ben, in the program and this is his first day. I'm going to show him around. It's a good program, but nobody on the staff seems to have time to give you a tour. They're all too busy with the kids."

Jim: "Hey, Rosa. It's great to meet someone else who uses the program."

Rosa: "Nice to meet you, Jim. Good luck finding out about what Ben does here. Beth is right when she says the staff doesn't seem to have time for the parents. I know they think I rush Lisha out of here, but they don't have time to talk, anyway. I don't really know much about what goes on. I wish the program had a newsletter. That would give me something to go on when I ask Lisha what she did all day."

Jim: "Well, I'm getting a little nervous about the supervision here. I'm not sure the staff knows what goes on between the kids. Ben's eleven and I think he gets a lot of pressure from other kids to waste money. Last night, he said all his friends were getting $150 sneakers for playing on the basketball team at the program. I'm raising him on my own and I don't have that kind of money. I'm also raising a teenager who's always testing me. I'm never sure where she is or what she's doing after school. We used to be great buddies, but now we're constantly arguing. By the time everybody is home and under control, I'm ready to crash. I'm not sure a newsletter would help me find out what's happening with my kids. Besides, all I do all day long is analyze reports. The last thing I need at night is a newsletter to read!"

Beth: "Really? We both think it would be great to have a newsletter. We'd read every word. I'd even like it if they could send it via e-mail. Then I could read it on a break at work."

Jim: "Well, not me. I'd rather hear what's going on face to face. Then I could ask questions about what Ben does here and how he feels about the place and the other kids! I'm nervous about losing touch with Ben now that he's getting older. I don't want to have the same relationship with him that I have with my daughter. I'm really scared about what may happen to her, given the kids she hangs out with."

Beth: "I have the same feeling; Katie is getting so independent it almost scares me! And her older sister has changed overnight — she's become obsessed with makeup and fashion. And sometimes she acts like she doesn't want to be seen with me and she's just plain rude. It just drives me nuts! Katie is starting to copy her. But anyway, Jim, you can really tell a lot about the program, just by looking around. I don't always know what Katie does all day, but I look for signs that the place is clean, safe and comfortable. Even the noise level tells me something. If it's too loud, it grates on my nerves and I think it would irritate Katie, too — especially if she's trying to get her homework done."

Jim: "Oh, I don't know. Noise doesn't really bother me. I used to teach, and I can tell if it's 'good noise' or 'bad noise.' Kids who are busy doing things they like can make a lot of good noise, but kids who aren't happy and aren't getting along can make a lot of bad noise!"

Rosa: "You were a teacher, Jim? Then maybe you can give the staff here some tips on how to keep the kids organized and under control. The place seems chaotic at times."

Jim: "Do you really think so, Rosa? I kind of like the idea that the kids have the freedom to do what they want to do. It makes it feel like home. I think Ben needs to blow off some steam after school, rather than being told what to do all the time. I know what it's like in the classroom! I will say this, though, it sounds like both of you have different ideas about what's going on here and what you want for your kids."

Rosa: "We probably do want different things. After all, our kids are different from each other. When I think about it, no one has ever really asked me what I want for Lisha. Has anyone ever asked your opinion, Beth?"

Beth: "Not really. And I don't feel comfortable making suggestions. One time I did make a comment about how messy the art area was. It irritates me to see supplies wasted because I pay a lot of money for Katie to go here. Plus, I don't want her to waste things — we're very frugal and neat at home. The staff person — I don't know her name — told me the kids must not have to put their things away at home. I couldn't believe it; it seemed like she was blaming me for the mess in the art area!"

Rosa: "You know, sometimes they make me feel guilty, too. When you said you didn't know the name of the staff person who put you down, I realized I've never been introduced to two of the new staff who are here at the end of the day. Have they told you their names?"

Beth: "No. How about you, Jim? Have you met the staff?"

Jim: "No. I just met the coordinator; she told me the names of the other staff, but I can't remember them. I have a hard time remembering names if I can't put them with a face. But like I said earlier, I not only want to know about the staff, I want to see what the kids are like who go here. I'm hoping Ben won't pick up with any troublemakers. He can have a bad temper, at times!"

Rosa: "Well, it's getting late; let's go in and see what's going on. It's been great talking with you both; I just wish we could have been relaxing with a cup of coffee instead of leaning on our cars in the parking lot!

Beth: "Me too!"

65

DISCUSSION QUESTIONS FOR WHAT DO PARENTS REALLY WANT? SKIT:

1. What were some of the things these parents wanted from their school-age program? What similar concerns did they have? What different or conflicting concerns or interests did they have? What issues or challenges were they facing?

2. How does this school-age program relate to other events and experiences in the lives of these parents?

3. Based on the parents' comments, how well do you think their school-age program is meeting their individual needs, interests and concerns? Cite examples.

4. What actions could the school-age program take that would be supportive and helpful to these parents? That is, what steps could the program take to be more family-friendly?

5. Which of the parents' comments related to the tasks of the *Interpretive* and/or *Interdependent Stages* of parenthood? (See the following questions related to each Stage.)

For the Interpretive Stage…..
- What signs did you see that the parents are coping with issues related to what kind of life they want to provide for their children?

- What signs did you see that parents may be trying to decide how they want their children to behave?

- What signs did you see that parents may be trying to decide how to interpret facts or experiences or standards to their children?

- What signs did you see that parents are dealing with how much to step in and do things with their children?

- What signs did you see that parents want to connect with other significant people in their children's lives?

- What signs did you see that parents are working on defining the changing relationship between parent and child?

- What things could staff do to help parents with tasks of the Interpretive Stage?

For the Interdependent Stage…..
- What signs did you see that parents are re-examining their images of who their children are becoming?

- What signs did you see that parents are coping with understanding the stages of adolescence?

- What signs did you see that parents are struggling with finding new ways to communicate effectively with a changing teenager?

- What signs did you see that parents are trying to clarify their own standards and expectations for their teenagers?

- What signs do you see that parents are struggling with setting limits and giving guidance to their teenagers?

- What things could staff do to help parents with tasks of the Interdependent Stage?

6. Some parents are facing the challenge of moving between the tasks of the Interpretive Stage and the Interdependent Stage. How could staff provide support and help for parents who are facing this challenge?

Trainer Notes for Segment #2: Identifying Parent Wants

In Segment #2, staff discuss the "wants" of parents in their programs. They also participate in a small group activity to explore parent wants, interests, needs and concerns in more detail. Read the following to introduce this training segment.

> In the previous training segment we explored the wants, needs and concerns of Rosa, Beth and Jim. Let's think about the extent to which parents in your program might have some of the same wants, needs, interests and concerns as Rosa, Beth and Jim.

Invite staff to share their thoughts about the similarities and differences between the wants, needs, interests and concerns of Rosa, Beth and Jim and those of the parents in their program. Use the following questions to facilitate a discussion:

- If you do see similarities, how well are you addressing these issues?

- What family-friendly actions, policies and resources are in place to support the wants, needs, interests and concerns of parents in your program? What additions or improvements do you think are needed?

- What signs do you see that parents in your program are grappling with the tasks of the *Interpretive* or *Interdependent Stages of Parenthood?* Are some of your parents also working through other stages of parenthood? For example, in addition to school-age children, do they also have an infant or toddler (Nurturing Stage), a preschool child (Authority Stage), a child going off to college (Departure Stage)? What could your program do to support parents as they work through the tasks associated with different stages of parenthood?

- If you're not sure what wants, needs, interests and concerns exist among parents in your programs, how could you find out?

After discussing the questions, introduce the small group activity:

> In the next activity, you will work in small groups to 1) review a survey list of typical parent wants and interests, 2) evaluate which wants on the list exist among parents in your program, and 3) brainstorm ideas for addressing these wants and interests in your programs. The sample list of parent "wants" was collected from a wide variety of parents in many school-age programs across the country.

*Divide staff into small groups of four to six. Distribute the handout: **Sample List of What Parents Want from School-Age Programs** that begins on the next page. Review the instructions for the activity that appear on the handout. Allow about fifteen minutes for group work. Then, convene the larger group to share perspectives and ideas, using the **Discussion Questions** on the last page of the handout to facilitate the discussion.*

CORE LEARNING ACTIVITY FIVE

Sample List of What Parents Want
from School-Age Programs

INSTRUCTIONS

The following list of parent "wants" was collected from a variety of parents in school-age programs across the country. Before working as a group, have each group member take a few moments to rate each item. As you review the list, circle the appropriate number from 1 to 4 to help you assess the feelings of the parents in your program. Circle **1** if you think most parents have this want, **2** if you think some parents have this want, **3** if you think no parents have this want, and **4** if you're not sure whether parents in your program have this want. Once you've rated each "want" on the list use the space provided to add additional "wants."

When each group member has rated all items on the list, come together as a group to share and compare your views, using the **Discussion Questions** on the last page of the handout as a guide.

List of Parent "Wants"	*How Parents in Your Program Feel About the "Want"*
1. I want the staff to treat my child as an individual — to know his/her name and to help him/her develop his/her unique talents and abilities.	1 2 3 4
2. I want the hours to be convenient to my work schedule.	1 2 3 4
3. I want the program to have reasonable fees.	1 2 3 4
4. I want the program to keep me informed about what my child does every day.	1 2 3 4
5. I want the program to give me information about what activities are planned.	1 2 3 4
6. I want the program to be a clean, safe place so that I can know my child is healthy and safe when I'm not there.	1 2 3 4
7. I want the program to see to it that my child gets his/her homework done.	1 2 3 4
8. I want the staff to help my child learn skills and develop some hobbies.	1 2 3 4

9. I want the program to expand its services to include longer hours and/or more days.   1   2   3   4

10. I want the program to help me get to know other parents.   1   2   3   4

11. I want the program to provide a lot of interesting, exciting activities for my child.   1   2   3   4

12. I want the program to give my child a lot of time to play games and enjoy the outdoors.   1   2   3   4

13. I want the staff in the program to be well-qualified and well-trained.   1   2   3   4

14. I want the staff in the program to know how to guide and discipline children effectively.   1   2   3   4

15. I want the program to provide my child with nutritious snacks.   1   2   3   4

16. I want the program to be a place where my child feels comfortable and welcome.   1   2   3   4

17. I want the program staff to be kind, patient and understanding with my child.   1   2   3   4

18. I want the staff to keep me informed about any problems my child might be having.   1   2   3   4

19. I want the staff to ask for input about my child's needs and interests.   1   2   3   4

20. I want the staff to be friendly to me and give me a greeting when I arrive.   1   2   3   4

21. I want the staff to invite me to participate in the program in some way.   1   2   3   4

22. I want the program to solicit my advice and opinions about program policies and procedures.   1   2   3   4

23. I want the program to have a gathering place for parents to get information and visit with each other.   1   2   3   4

24. I want the staff to help my child make friends with other children.   1   2   3   4

25. I want the program to help my child connect with the community and take field trips.   1   2   3   4

26. I want the program to provide my child with information
to help him/her respect his/her body; stay drug free;
avoid alcohol, cigarettes and other harmful substances,
and live a healthful life style.

1 2 3 4

27. I want the program to help my child get involved in service
projects to help other people.

1 2 3 4

28. I want the program to help my child deal appropriately
with boy/girl issues.

1 2 3 4

29. I want the program to help me plan for emergency
situations (for example, late arrivals because of car breakdowns,
traffic jams, bad weather).

1 2 3 4

30. I want the program to help me locate community and
professional resources that can help me with family problems.

1 2 3 4

Use the space below to add additional "Wants" of parents in your program.

Additional Parent Wants

**How Parents in Your
Program Feel about the
Want (Rate from 1 – 4)**

Discussion Questions:

After completing your rating of how parents in your program feel about different "wants," (those on the list and those you've added), discuss the following questions in your group:

1. Do you and your colleagues have the same perceptions of what parents want from your program? If not, what accounts for the differences?

2. Looking at all the items you and your colleagues rated with a "1," ask the following questions:

   - Which ones are being accommodated in your program?

   - Which ones are not being accommodated in your program? What, if anything, could you do to make some accommodation?

Now, do the same for all items you rated with a "2."

3. Looking at all the items you rated with a "3," discuss whether you wish parents did have some of these "wants." If "yes," what are some things you could do to encourage them to have these "wants"?

4. Looking at all the items you rated with a "4," ask yourself how you could find out parents' feelings about these items.

Trainer Notes for Segment #3: Family-Friendly Game

*Throughout the first five **Core Learning Activities**, staff explored a wide variety of ideas for creating a program atmosphere that is welcoming, helpful and supportive to parents — an atmosphere that views parents as partners and is family-friendly. In Segment #3, staff participate in a brainstorming game to generate an extensive list of family-friendly actions their programs could implement.*

Divide participants into small groups of two or three for the activity. Then, use the following material to introduce the activity.

> We've been exploring a wide range of ideas for creating a family-friendly atmosphere in our programs. In this learning activity, you'll work in small groups to brainstorm a list of family-friendly actions for our program. Examples of family-friendly actions might be: calling parents by name, making a point of smiling at parents, asking parents regularly for input about their child's needs or setting up a parent suggestion box. You will have five minutes to list as many family-friendly actions as possible. If the whole group comes up with more than 30 different actions, there will be a group prize!

*(**Note:** Select a number goal that seems realistic for your group based on your program size, number of training participants, etc. Offer a prize such as a staff pizza party, special breakfast or lunch or another event or treat your staff would enjoy!).*

Give a signal to start the brainstorming. After 5 minutes, reconvene the larger group and have groups share two family-friendly actions from their lists. Record each action on chart paper to create a master list. After the first group shares two ideas, instruct each new group to contribute actions that are <u>not already listed on the master list</u>. Have each group continue sharing ideas until all groups have shared all ideas on their lists. Did you reach your goal?

To summarize the activity, facilitate a brief discussion of the following questions:

- Which ideas on the list do you like best?

- Which ideas could you implement right away?

- Which ideas could be implemented with further thought and planning?

CORE LEARNING ACTIVITY SIX

Responding to Parents with Special Concerns and Needs

PRELIMINARY NOTES

The first five **Core Learning Activities** focused on helping staff examine their perspectives on parents and develop awareness, knowledge and deeper understanding of parents of children in their programs. This awareness, knowledge and increased understanding can provide the foundation for reaching out to parents as resourceful partners with programs. When staff make a genuine effort to be family friendly, experience has shown that most parents can and will reciprocate in positive ways. The vast majority of parents want to be a part of their children's lives and support the efforts of those who care for and guide children and youth as they grow and mature.

However, there are times when parents are facing or involved in great challenges or problems. Some parents exhibit incredible resilience and resourcefulness and have built-in support systems that help them cope effectively under dire circumstances. Other parents find that these challenges and problems make it difficult, if not impossible, to be an effective parent or to connect with caregivers and youth workers in positive ways. While it is beyond the scope of this book to address specific strategies for working with parents who are involved in extremely difficult challenges or circumstances, it is important to acknowledge that these parents exist and that they need attention, help and support. It is important not only because we want to help the parent, but because when parents are suffering or unable to cope, families can crumble and children suffer.

While program staff may want to be helpful to parents facing extreme challenges, they often do not have the expertise, background, experience or training to provide this help on their own. For the most part, staff in out-of-school programs are not social workers, nor should they be expected to act as if they were. At the same time, staff often are the first people who come face to face with parents and families who are truly struggling on a daily basis and don't know where to turn. To be effective with these parents, staff need guidance, information, support and assistance from supervisors or other professionals. Armed with useful information and appropriate guidance from other professionals, frontline staff in out-of-school programs often can become facilitators who help families connect with resources that can provide the help and support they need. With this in mind, this final **Core Learning Activity** is focused on two areas: 1) helping staff identify some of the most challenging situations that are, or may be, affecting parents in their programs; and 2) exploring ways staff can gather information and identify human, institutional and community resources that can help them cope with challenging situations in the best way possible. This learning activity includes large and small group discussion.

Number of Participants: Any number

Trainer Resources:

Gather the following before the session:

Phone books from the local community (two for each small group of 4 to 6 participants)

Brochures from community agencies that provide information and support for parents and families experiencing difficult challenges (for example, social services, health departments, youth agencies, departments of extension, cultural heritage organizations and non-profit organizations that focus on particular problems or specific populations — homelessness, substance abuse and alcoholism, services for immigrant workers, grief counseling, support groups related to health issues, etc.)

An assortment of catalogs with recommended books for after-school programs (for example, School-Age NOTES and other catalogs featuring materials for school-age programs — at least two catalogs for each group).

Books or lists recommending the best books for children and/or best books for adults on specialized topics (contact your local or school librarian for current titles)

Handout: CLA6-1 *Helping Parents in Difficult or Challenging Circumstances*

Time needed: 2 hours

Space: Area with tables and chairs for small group work

CONDUCTING THE ACTIVITY

*Use the **Preliminary Notes** (see previous page) to introduce the **Core Learning Activity**. Tell participants they will work in small groups to 1) identify some of the special challenges that are, or may be, affecting parents in their programs, and 2) explore ideas and resources for providing help and support to parents who may be having difficulty coping with challenging situations. Divide participants into groups of four to six. Distribute the handout: **Helping Parents in Difficult or Challenging Circumstances**. Review the instructions on the handout and allow about one hour for small group work. After an hour, reconvene the large group to share ideas. Use the questions at the end of the handout as a guide for facilitating sharing and discussion.*

***Note:** During the large group discussion, it is important to acknowledge that working effectively with parents who are experiencing difficult challenges can be very stressful for staff. An integral part of planning ways to help parents should include how to provide emotional support to staff to guard against exhaustion and burnout.*

Close the session by selecting one initiative that staff could take to support the needs of parents and families in challenging situations. Develop an Action Plan. Follow up with additional initiatives.

CORE LEARNING ACTIVITY SIX

Helping Parents in Difficult or Challenging Circumstances

INSTRUCTIONS

Review the following list of challenging situations, circumstances and problems that might affect the parents of children and youth in school-age programs. Identify which items on the list are, or may be, affecting parents and families you serve. Next, add additional situations, circumstances or problems that you think parents in your program may be experiencing. When your list is complete, discuss the questions on the next page of the handout.

1. Currently going through a divorce
2. Involved in a lawsuit over custody of child(ren)
3. Sharing custody of child(ren)
4. Coping with a chronic disease
5. Coping with a fatal disease
6. Coping with a death of a family member (for example, child, spouse, sibling, parent) or death of someone close to the family (boss, colleague, neighbor, family friend)
7. Recently lost a job
8. Coping with extreme financial difficulties (for example, evictions, foreclosures)
9. Homelessness
10. Defendant in a court case
11. Incarcerated
12. Military deployment or extended travel because of work or other family responsibilities
13. Victim of a crime
14. Victim of racial prejudice or other biases
15. Involved in substance abuse or living with someone who is
16. Responsible for supporting and/or caring for extended family members (for example, elderly parent, sibling)
17. Abusive parent or living with someone else who is abusive

18. Parent of a child with special needs (for example, children with physical disabilities, ADD, chronic illnesses and other challenging conditions)

19. Immigrant parent (with legal or illegal status)

20. Parent of a foster child

21. Parent of an adopted child

22. Parent who does not speak English or for whom English is not the primary language

23. Experiencing conflicts related to cultural background, economic background, religious beliefs, lifestyle and/or social choices

Other challenges, stresses or unique issues facing parents in your program:

Discussion Questions:

1. What resources (for example, human resources, institutional resources and print and media resources) are available to help staff support and work effectively with parents experiencing the challenges you identified?

2. What information is available on your program's parent bulletin board, in a parent newsletter or in a parent library (for example, books, magazines, videos, etc.) that would help parents who are experiencing the challenges you identified? What types of information could be made available through a bulletin board, newsletter or library to help parents who haven't shared special concerns or may not be ready to ask for help?

3. What books are available in the children's library area that would be appropriate and helpful for children who are living in families who are experiencing the challenges you identified? What types of books should be added to the children's library? What are the best ways to identify appropriate books? (Refer to resources provided for this activity.)

4. What community resources could be accessed to help staff work more effectively with parents and families who are experiencing the challenges you've identified? (Refer to brochures, phone books and other resources provided for this activity.)

5. What community partners could join your program in providing help and support to parents and families experiencing the challenges you've identified (for example, schools, social services, youth agencies, churches and synagogues, tribal councils, medical associations, etc.)? What is the best and most appropriate way to approach these potential community partners?

6. What educational opportunities could be provided to help staff understand and respond effectively to parents who are experiencing the challenges you've identified? (for example, special speakers and/or workshops, books, films, on-line courses, interactive Web sites, etc.).

2

Assessing the Needs, Interests and Concerns of Parents
(Tools to Use in Your Program)

Introduction to Section Two

Section Two contains a variety of tools to help staff and administrators learn more about the parents and families they serve. Five types of tools are included:

1. Sample posters focused on reaching out to parents and encouraging them to share important ideas and information with staff.

2. Sample letters to parents and related forms for collecting information and soliciting parent feedback.

3. A general tip sheet with a variety of ideas for soliciting suggestions and input from parents.

4. Tip sheets for sharing information with parents through parent bulletin boards, Web sites and newsletters.

5. Sample surveys for soliciting parents' opinions about the program.

The materials in **Section Two** can be used to supplement learning activities in **Section One**. They can also be used to create additional learning activities related to assessing and responding effectively to the needs, interests and concerns of parents.

Creating Family-Friendly Posters

Create a family-friendly poster for your program to solicit ideas, suggestions, concerns and important information related to different issues and program areas. Decorate the posters by hand or on the computer, using a catchy theme. To add appeal to parents, invite children to help decorate the poster. Place the poster near the entrance of your program where parents can see it daily.

Three sample posters are provided on the following pages.

Version One

This version uses a music motif and the phrase "Help us stay in tune with your needs and interests" to solicit parent input in eight areas. This poster could remain up throughout the year as a reminder that you're always open to listening to parents.

Version Two

This version uses a puzzle motif and the phrase "Help us match up with your needs and interests" to solicit parent input related to four selected areas. This poster could be displayed for a month or two, and then replaced with a fresh poster related to other areas.

Version Three

This version uses a train motif and the phrase "Help Us Stay on Track to Serve You Better," to solicit parent input related to four selected areas. This poster could be displayed for a month or two, and then replaced with a fresh poster related to other areas you want to emphasize.

ADDITIONAL TIPS

- *You will notice that Version One of the poster requests parent input in eight areas. Rather than listing all eight areas on one poster you may want to create a different poster for each area. Then use the posters to decorate a hallway or a wall near the parent bulletin board. Or, display a different poster each month. That way, you'll keep introducing ways parents can provide feedback throughout the year!*

- *Along with suggesting areas for parent input, be sure to emphasize your commitment to building relationships with parents on every poster, using some of the phrasing on the samples (for example, "We have a commitment to family-friendly service." "We want to build positive relationships with all of our families. Help us achieve our goal!" "Visit whenever you can — you are always welcome!")*

- *Choose a motif or theme for decorating each poster. For example, in addition to the motifs used in the samples, you might have other themes such as: Help Us "Stay in Touch" (use hand motifs), Help Us "Build Connections" (various building motifs), "Help Us Stay in Gear" (connecting cog and gear motifs).*

Help us stay in tune with your needs and interests

WE HAVE A COMMITMENT TO FAMILY-FRIENDLY SERVICE...

To Keep Our Commitment, We Need Your Help Throughout the Year!

♪ Tell us about your day when you pick up your child.

♪ Help us learn about your child's special talents and strengths.

♪ Tell us when your child needs extra help or support.

♪ Keep us informed about any important changes we need to know about to serve you well.

♪ Let us know about your family and cultural traditions.

♪ Make suggestions when you think we could serve you better.

♪ Ask us questions if you don't understand our policies and procedures.

♪ Tell us how you would like to connect with your child's experience in the program.

VISIT WHENEVER YOU CAN — YOU ARE ALWAYS WELCOME!

We want to build positive relationships with all of our families...
Help us achieve this goal!

PARENTS!

HELP US MATCH UP

WITH

YOUR NEEDS & INTERESTS

- Tell us about your day when you pick up your child.

- Help us learn about your child's talents and interests.

- Let us know about your family and cultural traditions.

- Tell us how you would like to connect with your child's experience in the program.

We want to build positive relationships with all of our families. Help us achieve this goal!

VISIT WHENEVER YOU CAN — YOU ARE ALWAYS WELCOME!

Get on board, parents!

School-Age NOTES

HELP US STAY ON TRACK TO SERVE YOU BETTER!

WE WANT TO BUILD POSITIVE RELATIONSHIPS WITH ALL OF OUR FAMILIES!

HELP US ACHIEVE THIS GOAL!

- Tell us when your child needs extra help or support.

- Keep us informed about any important changes we need to know about to serve you well.

- Make suggestions when you think we could serve you better.

- Ask us questions if you don't understand our policies and procedures.

VISIT WHENEVER YOU CAN. YOU ARE ALWAYS WELCOME!

Cover Letters and Forms for Collecting Information from Families

Two sets of **Cover Letters** and **Information Collecting Forms** appear on the following pages. These materials are designed to collect different types of information about children, parents and families. Both sets can provide valuable information for you and your staff about the families you serve.

Cover Letter and Response Form — Set One focuses on 1) soliciting information to help you understand each child's interests and needs and 2) to learn about how parents prefer to connect with their child's experience in your program.

Cover Letter and Response Form — Set Two encourages families to share information about their cultural background to help you create a positive atmosphere for cultural diversity and sharing.

Important Note: If your program serves parents and families whose primary language is not English, explore options for having the letter and forms printed in other languages. You may also want to consider securing the assistance of a translator to help some parents complete the forms.

SAMPLE COVER LETTER AND RESPONSE FORM — SET ONE

(Tell us about your child and tell us about your needs, interests, and preferences)

Dear Parent,

We are happy you have chosen our (school-age/after school, etc.) program for your child. We want to do our very best to provide an environment where your child will feel safe, happy and valued. We also want you to feel comfortable here and connected to what your child experiences each day.

To provide the best possible experiences for your child, we need input from you about your child's needs, interests and personal style and about your family needs and preferences. We've enclosed a form to help you share important information about your child and family. The form is divided into two parts. Please help us build a great partnership with you by completing **Part One** and **Part Two**.

- **Part One** will help us gain an understanding of your child's needs, interests and personal style. This information will help us do our best to help your child feel good about being here.

- **Part Two** will help us understand more about your needs, interests and preferences as a parent. We are committed to understanding our parents' needs and building an ongoing positive relationship with each family. We know that today's families often are experiencing many pressures and demands on their time. With this in mind, we would like to know your preferences about the best ways for you to connect with your child's program.

If you have questions about the form or need help in completing it, please let us know. *Let's work together to build the best possible connection between you, your child and the program!*

Sincerely,

Director, XYZ School-Age Program

PART ONE: *TELL US ABOUT YOUR CHILD*

Basic information

Name of Child _____ Birthdate _____

Prefers to be called _____ Grade _____

Child's Primary Language _____

Mother's Home Phone # _____ Office # _____

Father's Home Phone # _____ Office # _____

OR, if applicable:

Guardian Phone # _____ Office # _____

- -

Information about your child's interests

First, tell us about your child's favorite activities to do at home or in the neighborhood. Check all the activities that your child enjoys. Then list examples of your child's favorite activities in the space provided below.

___sports and outdoor games   ___board and table games   ___dancing/singing

___arts and crafts   ___playing a musical instrument   ___computers

___listening to music   ___exploring nature   ___reading

___building things   ___socializing with friends   ___play acting

___cooking   ___working on a special hobby   ___other (list below)

Examples of your child's favorite activities (List specific games, sports, crafts, musical instruments, hobbies, etc.)

_____

_____

_____

Are there activities your child has not had a chance to do at home, but might like to try in the program? (Check Yes or No) ___Yes ___No

If you checked "Yes," please list them here:

_____

_____

_____

(continued on next page)

SECTION TWO

(continued from page 87)

Information about your child's temperament and personal style

Although we all have a lot in common, each of us is unique! Please tell us a little about your child's temperament and personal style so that we can provide appropriate guidance and support to your child as an individual.

For example, is your child **active**? **quiet**? **shy**? **outgoing**? **intense**? **easygoing**? **persistent**? **distractible**? Please use the space below to tell us a little about your child's characteristics.

What do you think are your child's best qualities?

What are the ***most important things we can do*** to help your child have a positive experience in our school-age program? Are there areas where you feel your child may need any kind of extra help or support? If yes, please describe them.

*Thank you for telling us about your child! Now go to **Part Two** and tell us about your needs, interests and preferences!*

_____

_____

_____

_____

_____

_____

_____

_____

_____

_____

_____

_____

_____

_____

_____

_____

_____

_____

_____

_____

Part Two: *Tell Us about Your Needs, Interests and Preferences...*

We want to share information with you about our program and about your child's experience in the program. Please comment on how you would like us to share information with you. For example, do you like to…(check one or all)

_____ read newsletters and bulletin boards?

_____ receive notes and/or phone calls about your child's experiences?

_____ attend informational meetings or workshops on parenting?

_____ visit a program Web site?

_____ receive information via e-mail?

_____ other ideas?

Your comments...

We value your opinions and ideas about program policies and procedures. If you would like to share your opinions and ideas with us, please comment on how you would like to do this. For example, would you like to…(check one or all)

_____ serve on parent advisory committees or boards?

_____ participate in opinion surveys?

_____ attend policy forums?

_____ use a suggestion box?

_____ other ideas?

Your comments...

We welcome parents' participation during program hours. If you want to participate, tell us the best way(s) for you to do so. For example, would you like to…(check one or all)

_____ share a special skill or hobby?

_____ lead a special club?

_____ go on a field trip?

_____ help out where needed on occasion?

_____ other ideas?

Your comments...

We value having parents assist us behind the scenes. Please let us know if you would like to help us develop, gather or repair resources for the program. For example, could you help with…

_____ fundraising?

_____ printing the newsletter?

_____ repairing broken equipment?

_____ locating recyclable items for use in the program?

_____ other ideas?

Your comments...

We like to help organize special services to help parents whenever possible. Here are some services we are considering. Check any of the services that you might like to use. Also, check the space to the right of each service if you would like to help with organization.

Might Use	Service	Interest in Organizing
_____	A business-card swap among program parents	_____
_____	A buddy system with other parents who could help out in emergencies	_____
_____	Children's clothing swaps or sales	_____
_____	Swaps or sales of used toys and games	_____
_____	A baby-sitting co-op among program parents	_____
_____	Support groups for parents with similar concerns	_____
	(What type of support group would interest you? _____)	
_____	A family and community events calendar	_____
_____	Other ideas	_____

Please describe other idea(s): _____

_____

_____

_____

Sample Cover Letter and Response Form - Set Two

(Learning about family backgrounds, customs and experiences – family history questionnaire)*

Dear Parent,

One goal of our school-age program is for the children to learn to appreciate and accept all people as a result of their daily experiences with each other, especially during the time they spend together in our program. We know that our families have a variety of backgrounds, customs, histories, traditions, occupations and experiences.

I am asking that you share information about your family's cultural background. This will provide a valuable resource for our program in creating an atmosphere of cultural diversity. We will use the information you provide in program planning, giving the children an opportunity to study and role-play the customs and lifestyles of their friends as well as those of their own culture. When children (and adults) understand the feelings and beliefs of their friends, respect for others is the byproduct. In addition, children develop an appreciation and further understanding of their own family traditions.

If you are willing to share your family's culture with us, please answer the questions on the following page and return to me by (day/date). If you have questions or need help completing the form, please let us know.

Your responses will be posted on a large mural in the entrance to the program unless you request that they not be posted. To make our mural more interesting, children will create illustrations of your responses. We also will be taking photos of families at pick-up time over the next two weeks and will add them to the display.

We hope you will be enthusiastic about sharing your family's traditions with us! Be on the lookout for a great mural that shares the traditions of all of our beautiful families!

Sincerely,

Director, XYZ School-Age Program

* Adapted with permission from Patrick Air Force Base School-Age Child Care Program, Patrick Air Force Base, Florida. Lynn Phillips, program director; Tony Boob, youth center director

FAMILY HISTORY QUESTIONNAIRE

Please answer the following as they apply to your family. Use additional pages if necessary.

1. **Family name:** _____

2. **Child's full name:** _____

3. These countries, cultures, are represented in our family:

    _____
    _____
    _____

4. Some of the holidays, celebrations, customs, traditions, etc., that we observe are:

    _____
    _____
    _____

5. Select one of the holidays, traditions and/or customs that your family observes and explain how you observe it (what activities you do, what food you eat, etc.):

    _____
    _____
    _____

6. Tell us about the music, dress and/or artifacts that are a part of your family culture:

    _____
    _____
    _____

7. What languages or dialects are spoken in your family?

    _____
    _____
    _____

8. Tell us about some of the different occupations and professions represented in your family:

_____

_____

_____

9. What are some of the foods that represent your family's culture? What foods are your family's favorite to prepare and eat?

_____

_____

_____

10. Please share one of your family's favorite stories, one that is always told when you get together with other family members.

_____

_____

_____

11. Tell us about any other special things you would like to share about your family.

_____

_____

_____

Please attach additional pages if necessary to complete your comments.

How to Solicit Ongoing Suggestions from Parents

It is great to get input from parents when they enroll their children, but that's only the beginning. Building positive relationships with parents is an ongoing process. An important part of building such relationships is encouraging parents to give you feedback and ideas throughout the year. A few ideas for soliciting ongoing suggestions from parents:

Informal daily conversations with parents. When parents drop off or pick up their children, don't miss the opportunity to extend a friendly greeting and share something about the child's day. During informal exchanges with parents, ask for their ideas and suggestions whenever possible. Some programs assign one staff person to greet parents toward the end of the day. This staff person can devote full attention to assisting parents, asking them about their day and listening to any suggestions they might have to offer. If you implement this procedure, be sure to let parents know which staff member has this responsibility (and which staff are expected to stay focused on children and youth). For example, the "parent greeter" might wear a "parent greeter" badge. In a large program, a different staff member might be the "parent greeter" every day, giving parents an opportunity to interact with all staff.

Listen to what children say about their parents' interests, talents, hobbies, etc. Then, follow up with phone calls and informal conversations with parents. Invite them to contribute ideas in areas where they have interests and expertise.

Conduct telephone surveys. Develop a brief list of open-ended questions and solicit parent suggestions and opinions about various aspects of your program over the phone. Let parents know you will be doing this and ask them to let you know if they prefer not to participate in a telephone survey.

Display a parent suggestion box near the parent bulletin board or another spot that is clearly visible and accessible to parents. Invite children to help you decorate the box so that it is eye-catching and attractive. (**Note:** Children might like to have a suggestion box, too!) Post a friendly, brief notice near the box inviting parent suggestions. In the notice, let parents know they do not have to sign their suggestions. However, remind parents that it may be easier to follow-up on a suggestion if you can chat with the parent who made it. That way, you can clarify any questions you might have about the suggestion and have the opportunity to work together to implement the suggestion if possible. Remember, if you solicit suggestions, it is essential to let parents know what suggestions you've received and how you plan to respond. You can do this privately or publicly at a meeting, in a memo, etc. — whatever seems most appropriate. Even if you cannot act on all suggestions, it is important for parents to know that you've read them and considered them. Without feedback, parents will assume their ideas are disappearing into thin air, and they'll assume it is a waste of time to share them.

Host parent forums or discussion groups. Parent forums and discussion groups can be especially useful if you are grappling with specific difficult issues in your program (for example, funding cuts, high staff turnover or difficulty recruiting substitute teachers). These types of issues can have a direct effect on parents and parents can often help you work toward solutions where everyone benefits. In one program experiencing difficulty recruiting and retaining part-time staff, 75 parents who had been complaining about high staff turnover attended a forum to discuss the issue. After a briefing by the director, parents were asked to help brainstorm recruiting ideas. They came up with more than 50 ideas for recruitment that the staff had not tried. They also recommended that the program consider raising salaries to help recruit and retain staff!

Sponsor informal "get acquainted" coffees, pot-luck dinners or other social events for parents. Informal gatherings of parents provide an excellent opportunity to talk with parents about their suggestions and new ideas for enhancing and enriching the program.

Conduct an ongoing feedback survey. Place copies of a short survey soliciting feedback from parents in a large envelope and post the envelope on or near your parent bulletin board. Label the envelope: "Parent Survey – Please Complete One!" Post a notice next to the envelope, inviting parents to complete the survey whenever they would like to give you feedback about the program or make suggestions. Post a second envelope labeled "Completed Parent Surveys" nearby. Don't forget to read the completed surveys and get back to parents with your response! (**Note:** Keep the survey forms simple and short. See ongoing parent survey form later in **Section Two** for suggested survey format and open-ended questions.) **Alternative Survey Process:** If your program and program parents have access to the Internet, post your ongoing survey online so that parents can complete it at home or on a break at work. Search the Web for "creating online surveys" to locate sites such as www.SurveyMonkey.com where you can find help in creating your own online surveys.

Conduct Periodic Formal Surveys. Once or twice a year, distribute surveys that give parents in your program an opportunity to indicate how they feel about various aspects of your program. (See sample Parent Satisfaction Survey later in **Section Two**). If you have families in your program who do not speak English, include translations of the survey form in their primary language if at all possible. Post Parent Satisfaction Surveys online if parents and the program have access to the Internet.

Make ongoing feedback forms available. Encourage parents to give you feedback about various aspects of the program by providing feedback forms in envelopes on your parent bulletin board or on a table near where parents check in or out each day. *Feedback Forms* provide parents with a convenient vehicle for giving you feedback on ideas or problems and compliments. (See sample feedback forms later in **Section Two**.) Post feedback forms online if both parents and the program have access to the Internet.

Ideas for Parent Bulletin Boards and Web Sites

Display a parent bulletin board in a spot that is visible to parents as they come and go. If your program and program parents have access to the Internet, consider creating a Web site that serves as a parent bulletin board. Unless you are certain that all parents have access to the Internet, don't depend on the Web site parent bulletin board to get information out. Provide an in-house parent bulletin board and a Web site parent bulletin board. **Note:** Be sure to get releases from parents if posting photos on the site. Some ideas for developing the content of parent bulletin boards.

CONTENT

Include separate sections of information on a variety of topics. Examples of appropriate sections are listed below. Select sections that are most appropriate for parents in your program. Start with a few sections and topics, then add more as you learn more about parents' needs, interests and concerns.

What's happening: information about the program

- Samples of program brochures
- Registration information
- Copy of the current program newsletter
- Announcements about any changes in the calendar or schedule
- Weekly or monthly calendar of planned activity offerings, including a general schedule for the day
- News about club activities
- Photographs of children engaged in different activities: field trips, building with blocks, play acting in the drama area, reading, playing outdoor games, playing a board game, helping a friend, etc. Add an extra touch by including quotes by the children about what's going on in the photographs.
- Children's favorite jokes of the day or week
- Quotable quotes from children at work and play in the program
- Announcements of special upcoming events: parent get-togethers, parent advisory group meetings, performances by the children (talent shows, magic shows, etc.), appearances of special visitors from the community, etc.
- Announcements of parent workshops and seminars sponsored by the program
- Invitations for parent participation in specific activities
- Requests for contributions of recyclable materials for use in the program
- Requests for help in other areas of the program that could benefit from parent assistance or ideas

Community activities and other resources for parents

- Listings and pamphlets about professional resources and community agencies related to family living, health care, consumer assistance, family finances, etc.

- Community-sponsored workshop opportunities on topics of interest to parents: single parenting, separation and divorce, stress management, toy safety, guiding children's behavior, balancing work and family, etc.

- Community recreational opportunities for children and families

- Local happenings of interest to families in your community

- Book reviews on topics of interest to parents (for children and adults)

People-to-people news

Create this section to help parents, staff and supporters of the program get to know more about each other as people. Some ideas:

- Photos of staff members, including brief bios of their educational background and experience, as well as special hobbies and other leisure time interests

- Photos of families in the program, with brief descriptions of family interests, activities, traditions, parents' work activities, etc., provided by the parents and children. If space is an issue, make this a weekly feature, highlighting different families each week.

- Photos of people who provide your program with valued support and assistance: corporate donors, special visitors and regular volunteers. Invite each person to contribute a brief quote about why they support the program, how they feel about their experience at the program or why they feel the program is important to the community.

- News about parents in the program (for example, Ms. Jones named employee of the month; Mr. Sanchez receives master's degree; Mr. and Mrs. Kelly open a restaurant; Ms. Baker volunteers at community soup kitchen; Dr. Johnson speaks at medical convention). Ask children and parents regularly about their activities and accomplishments and feature as many parents as possible — with their permission, of course!

Give us your ideas and comments section

- Parent Feedback Forms: I Have an Idea, I Have a Compliment, I Have Problem

- Ongoing Parent Survey forms with a notice encouraging parents to complete these forms whenever they would like to comment on how the program is going.

- Comments section: Quotes from parents about the program (excerpted from I Have a Compliment Forms — when parents give you permission to share their comments)

FORMAT

If you plan to create and maintain a parent bulletin board within your program, refer to the suggestions that follow. They will help you develop a bulletin board that parents will want to stop and read. If you also plan to develop a Web site parent bulletin board that includes any or all of the sections described in previous pages, secure the services of a Web site designer. Once your Web site is up and operational, secure a Web master to manage your Web site. You may be able to locate a Web site designer and Web master who will donate their time to creating and maintaining a Web site for your program (for example, a parent who has skills in this area, a hobbyist, a firm specializing in Web site design that does some community pro bono work).

Tips for creating and maintaining an in-house parent bulletin board

- Secure a large space for the bulletin board so that items won't be crowded.

- Use fadeless paper as a background, if possible. It holds its color indefinitely so that you won't have to replace it as you remove items and change your bulletin board around. Use bold primary colors, but don't overpower the eye (for example, avoid fluorescent colors for the background).

- Create borders to enhance the overall appearance of the board and to separate each section. Use commercial border products that are fadeless and come in a variety of colors. Use children's artwork for extra interest.

- Label the board in letters 4 to 5 inches high. Place the label above or at the top of the bulletin board. Consider using letters cut from corrugated paper; it comes in a variety of colors and adds texture and interest to the bulletin board. Or, make a computer-generated banner using an attractive font and clip art.

- Mount photographs or notices on colored card stock to set them off.

- Highlight headings and important information in bright colors with markers to accent some items and spark curiosity.

- When posting information, start from the center of the board and work out. Remember to separate each major section so that information is easy to locate. Avoid straight lines or uniform rows that can make a board look dull and uninteresting. Use material that offers variety in size, shape and color. Fill the board with lots of information, but avoid overcrowding.

- Keep an ongoing file of information and keep the board fresh and up-to-date! Be sure to remove information about events that are over.

- Solicit help from one or more parents. Ask them to keep an eye out for interesting articles and events, help you create and maintain the board and help you generate new ideas about what parents would like to see on the bulletin board.

Ideas for Parent Newsletters

Make your own "good news" headlines! Create a bi-weekly or monthly parent newsletter to keep parents informed about what's happening in your program. Keep the newsletter short — one or two pages at most. If parents and the program have access to the Internet, post the parent newsletter on your program Web site or distribute the newsletter via e-mail. Some ideas of sections or columns to include in a newsletter for parents:

- Weekly or monthly calendar of planned activity offerings
- Announcements about any changes in the calendar or schedule
- Brief discussions about program philosophy, goals, objectives, policies and procedures — discussions to help parents understand why you do what you do
- Reports about favorite activities, trips, etc., written by children
- News about club activities
- Children's favorite jokes of the day or week
- Family riddle of the week or month
- Quotable quotes from children at work and play in the program
- Children's artwork — drawings or cartoons
- Announcements of upcoming events and meetings:
  - parent get-togethers
  - parent advisory group meetings
  - performances by the children
  - field trips
  - appearances of special visitors from the community
  - community events of interest to parents
- Announcements of parent workshops and seminars sponsored by the program
- Invitations for parent participation in specific activities
- Requests for contributions of recyclable materials for use in the program
- Requests for help in other areas of the program that could benefit from parent assistance or ideas
- Information about new staff or staff changes, including brief bios and special interests
- News about families in the program— accomplishments, awards, promotions, special trips, etc.
- Thank you announcements and acknowledgments to parents who share their ideas, comments, suggestions, resources and expertise with the program

Design a newsletter that is easy and inviting to read — lots of "white space," short paragraphs (just a few sentences), illustrations by the children, etc.

Suggestion: Have a parent newsletter and a parent bulletin board to increase the chance of connecting with all the parents in your program. Some parents will read the newsletter, others will check out the bulletin board, and some will take advantage of both.

Parent Feedback Forms*

I'VE GOT A COMPLIMENT!
I'VE GOT A PROBLEM!
I'VE GOT AN IDEA!

Use parent feedback forms as a tool for prompting parents to give feedback in specific areas. Place copies of each form in three separate large envelopes. Display the envelopes on or near your parent bulletin board. Label the envelopes as follows:

Envelope 1: "Please use this form to share your compliments. We love to hear from you when we're doing things right!"

Envelope 2: "Please use this form to share any problems with the program. We want to be aware of any problems you're experiencing and work with you to solve them."

Envelope 3: "Please use this form to share your ideas for improving or enhancing the program. We know the children and staff can benefit from your creative thinking!"

Provide additional envelopes nearby for depositing completed parent feedback forms. Don't forget to read completed parent feedback forms and get back to parents with your response! If your program and program parents have access to the Internet, post parent feedback forms on your Web site so that parents can complete forms at home or on a break at work.

Suggestion: *Reproduce these forms on three eye-catching colors.*

---

* *(Adapted with permission from feedback forms developed by Fran Sokol Simon, program director, All Saints' All Day Child Care Centers, now Wonders Child Care Center, Chevy Chase, Maryland)*

I'm a Parent and I've Got a Compliment!

Please pass it on! Use this form as a tool for passing your positive comments on to program staff. Just fill it out and leave it in the envelope posted on the parent bulletin board. If you prefer, you may fill it out at home and mail or e-mail it to the program.

It is not necessary for you to provide your name on the form. However, if you would like to be contacted to discuss the compliment, or you would like specific people to be aware that you're pleased with their work, please consider including your name. Please be aware that if any action is taken as a result of your comments, we may not be able to make you aware of the action if you do not include your name.

It is always rewarding to hear great things from parents about our program! We thank you for taking the time to express your support.

Name: _____ *(Optional)*

If you do include your name, please check the appropriate statement below:

____ You may contact me, but I prefer that my compliments and name be kept confidential.

____ I grant permission to discuss my compliments with the involved individuals, but do not share my name.

____ I grant permission to discuss my compliments and my name.

This wonderful thing has happened! Let me tell you about it!

_____
_____
_____
_____
_____
_____
_____

To encourage future occurrences of this wonderful thing, the program should:

_____
_____
_____

Thank you for the compliment!

I'm a Parent and I've Got a Problem I Cannot Seem to Solve!

Please share it with us. Use this form as a tool for informing us of any problem you have regarding our program (policies, procedures, leadership, staff, the facility, the activities or any other issues of concern) that you have not been able to solve. Just fill out the form and leave it in the envelope posted on the parent bulletin board. If you prefer, you may fill it out at home and mail or e-mail it to the program.

It is not necessary for you to provide your name on the form. However, we encourage you to include your name so that we may talk with you further as we work to solve the problem. Please be aware that if any action is taken as a result of your comments, it may be impossible to make you aware of the action if you do not include your name.

In discussing your problem, please be as specific as possible. You may attach extra pages if necessary.

Whenever possible, we encourage you to try to resolve problems directly with the individuals involved, but we are certainly happy to assist you when this approach does not seem to work. We always appreciate your candid input.

Name:_____*(Optional)*

If you do include your name, please check the appropriate statement below:

_____ You may contact me, but I prefer that my problems and name be kept confidential.

_____ I grant my permission to discuss my problems with the involved individuals, but do not share my name with them.

_____ I grant permission to discuss my problem with involved individuals and share my name with them.

Description of the problem:

_____
_____
_____
_____
_____
_____
_____
_____
_____

Please list additional items on the reverse side.

Steps I have taken to solve my problem:

_____

_____

_____

_____

_____

I have_____ or have not_____talked with anyone in the program about this problem.

To solve my problem I'd like the following to be done:

_____

_____

_____

_____

_____

_____

_____

_____

_____

_____

To avoid this problem in the future, I suggest that:

_____

_____

_____

_____

_____

_____

_____

_____

_____

Other comments:

_____

_____

_____

Thank you for your effort to help us improve our program services.

I'm a Parent and I've Got an Idea!

Don't keep it a secret! While your idea is hot, use this form to tell us about any idea you have for improving or enhancing our program. We love hearing about your ideas in person, but if you would like to get your ideas down on paper, this form is your opportunity! Just fill it out and leave it in the envelope posted on the parent bulletin board. If you prefer, you may fill it out at home and mail or e-mail it to the program.

It is not necessary for you to provide your name on the form. However, if you would like to explore your idea with us in person, please consider including your name.

Name:_____*(Optional)*

If you do include your name, please check the appropriate statement below:

____ *I prefer my idea be kept confidential.*

____ *I grant permission to share my idea, but not my name.*

____ *I grant permission to share my idea and my name.*

Description of your idea:

_____

_____

_____

_____

_____

This is a great idea because:

_____

_____

I have_____ or have not_____ spoken to anyone in the program about this idea.

Suggestions that will make this idea work:

_____

_____

I would_____ would not_____ volunteer to be part of a committee to make this great idea fly. If you would, please include your phone numbers:

Home (   )_____ Work (   ) _____

Thank you for taking the time to share your idea to help improve the program!

Cover Letter and Ongoing Parent Survey Form

Post ongoing parent survey forms in an envelope on your parent bulletin board or on a table near the entrance to the program. Provide another envelope nearby where parents can deposit completed surveys. If the program and program parents have access to the Internet, post the survey form on the program Web site. Display the following note along with the forms. (See suggestions for creating online surveys presented earlier in **Section Two** in *Soliciting Feedback from Parents*.)

Dear Parents:

We want to stay in touch with how you feel about our program throughout the year. Of course, we want you to feel free to talk with us about your ideas or concerns at any time. We also want to encourage you to jot your feelings down from time to time. We've provided these parent survey forms for this purpose. The form is short and easy to complete. Please use it any time you would like to give us general feedback about how well we are meeting your needs. You may deposit your completed form in the envelope provided or mail or e-mail it to the program.

Thanks for your input!

Program Director

Ongoing Parent Survey Form

Please give us your candid responses to the following questions:

1. What do you like best about the program?

   _____

   _____

   _____

2. What do you like least about the program?

   _____

   _____

   _____

3. What would you like to see changed about the program, if anything?

   _____

   _____

   _____

4. What do you want to be sure never changes about the program, if anything?

   _____

   _____

   _____

5. On a scale of 1 to 10 (with 1 being the lowest and 10 being the highest), how would you rate your satisfaction with the program services _____
   Comments, if any:

   _____

   _____

   _____

6. On a scale of 1 to 10 (with 1 being the lowest and 10 being the highest), how would you rate your satisfaction with the program staff _____
   Comments, if any:

   _____

   _____

   _____

Name: _____ *(Optional)*

Please include your name if you would like to discuss your comments with us.

Parent Satisfaction Survey and Cover Letter*

Use the survey on the next page as a written or telephone survey, depending on the needs and preferences of parents in your program. If your program and program parents have access to the Internet, post the survey form on your Web site or send it as an e-mail. Post an envelope where parents can deposit completed surveys.

Dear Parent:

Each year we survey parents in our program to learn how well they are satisfied with program services. Please take a few minutes to share your thoughts and feelings about your child's school-age program. Your comments will help us make improvements to the existing program and make plans for new program initiatives if needed.

The survey is confidential and does not require your signature. Please return the form to our office by_____. You may deposit the completed survey in the envelope provided on the parent bulletin board, or if you prefer, you may mail or e-mail it to the program.

Thank you for sharing your input and suggestions.

Sincerely,

Program Director

(Adapted with permission from Cornell Cooperative Extension, Monroe County, NY)

END OF YEAR (OR SEMI-ANNUAL) PARENT SATISFACTION SURVEY

Please indicate below which sessions your child attended:

_____ before school _____after school _____holiday program _____summer

Please rate the following questions as they relate to your child's participation in the program. For each item, circle the number that most closely represents your feeling or opinion based on the following rating scale:

very satisfied		OK		very unsatisfied
1	2	3	4	5

1. How would you rate your satisfaction with the program?   1 2 3 4 5

2. How would you rate your child's satisfaction with the program?   1 2 3 4 5

3. How would you rate health and safety conditions?   1 2 3 4 5

4. How would you rate quality of learning experiences?   1 2 3 4 5

5. How would you rate quality of recreational activities?   1 2 3 4 5

6. How would you rate convenience of location?   1 2 3 4 5

7. How would you rate hours of operation?   1 2 3 4 5

8. How would you rate cost of the program?   1 2 3 4 5

9. How would you rate the program's relationships with parents?   1 2 3 4 5

Please comment on the following questions:

10. What are the best things about the program?

   _____

   _____

11. How can we improve the program?

   _____

   _____

12. What additional programs and services for parents and families would you like to see offered by the program?

   _____

   _____

Other comments?

   _____

   _____

Making Connections with Parents
(Tip Sheets for Program Staff)

3

Introduction to Section Three

Section Three contains a variety of tip sheets with ideas for creating positive connections with parents. Mix and match the ideas provided as appropriate for your own program. Also, use the ideas to jump-start staff thinking to create additional ideas of their own. Jot down ideas in the spaces provided in each tip sheet.

The first tip sheet in **Section Three** focuses on a variety of initiatives staff can take to help parents feel welcome, accepted and valued. Additional tip sheets address the following areas:

1. How to help parents form strong, positive relationships with staff and with other parents and children in the program.

2. How to involve parents in sharing input that can help shape the program design, policies and operation.

3. How programs can serve as a link between parents and the child's school day.

In addition to the tip sheets, **Section Three** contains an article that emphasizes the importance of taking a systematic approach to building relationships with parents. It stresses the importance of maintaining ongoing communication with individual parents to share information and provides tips for sharing problems appropriately when they do occur.

The tip sheets and article in **Section Three** can be used to supplement learning activities in **Section One.** They can also be used as the foundation for brainstorming sessions or for additional learning activities related to creating opportunities for parents to connect with out-of-school programs.

Ideas for Helping Parents Feel Welcome, Accepted and Valued

Ideas to Get You Started ...

1. *Create a Parent Comfort Corner*

   Provide parents with a place to gather when they drop off or pick up their children. A parent comfort corner sends the message: "You're welcome here; make yourself comfortable and stay awhile." Try any or all of the following suggestions for setting up your parent comfort corner.

   - Locate the parent comfort corner in an area that is somewhat removed from the program activity areas, yet is close enough for parents to view and listen to what is going on in the program if they would like to do so. Make a banner or poster that labels the area parent comfort corner or another name that would be just right for parents in your program.

   - Provide a small table and chair where parents can pause to write a note, fill out a field trip form, write a tuition check, etc. Provide a small jar of pens (perhaps imprinted with your program's name, address and phone number). Consider setting up a coffee pot with hot water and a basket of supplies for instant coffee and tea on the table. To help cover expenses, provide a jar for donations if needed. **Note:** If hot water is provided, be sure to locate the pot in a safe place where it will not be in the path of children as they go about their work and play.

   - From time to time, provide special treats in the parent comfort corner. For example, after-work snacks made by the children in a special cooking club, Monday morning doughnuts on the first Monday of every month, etc. Again, provide a voluntary donations jar if necessary.

   - Depending on space available, provide two or three comfortable chairs or a small sofa where parents can sit and relax or chat with another parent. Use folding chairs if space is shared.

   - Set up a parent bulletin board in the parent comfort corner. Include information about your program, information about community events and parenting. Also include photos of families and selected feedback forms and other forms inviting parents to contribute ideas, share compliments or concerns, etc. See *Ideas for Parent Bulletin Boards and Web Sites* in **Section Two.**

   - Provide a basket of magazines related to family living and child rearing. Subscribe to one or two magazines and/or write staff and parents to contribute recent back issues when they are finished with them. Remove back issues monthly. Be sure to save pertinent articles for your files and displays!

2. *Display a family-friendly poster at the entrance to your program*

Publicize your commitment to being a family-friendly program by prominently displaying a family-friendly poster in a place where parents will be reminded of your commitment every day. See *Creating Family-Friendly Posters* in **Section Two.**

3. *Make a practice of extending a friendly greeting to parents every day*

Studies have shown that staff often pass up the opportunity to establish positive relationships with parents when children are brought to or picked up from the program. This happens because staff are so involved in other important activities they forget to look up and say a friendly "Hello." A few ideas to help you maximize opportunities to make parents feel welcome, accepted and valued in your program:

- Learn parents' names. Make a commitment to greeting them with their names and a smile whenever they come into the program.

- If you have a large program and several staff, consider assigning one staff member to act as a parent greeter at arrival or dismissal time. This can help ensure that all parents will be acknowledged and welcomed every day. In addition to acting as a greeter, this staff member can serve as a facilitator who helps parents who need information, need help locating their child's belongings, want to make an appointment to discuss ideas or concerns, etc. Rotate this responsibility among staff members so that everyone has an opportunity to interact with parents. (Remember, just because one person is assigned as an official greeter doesn't mean that other staff should not smile and say "Hello" as parents arrive.)

- Whenever time permits, take a moment to have an informal exchange with parents. Ask them about their day or their weekend, extend a compliment or inquire about a special family event their child has mentioned to you (arrival of a baby, acquisition of a new pet, visit from grandma, a recent trip or family celebration).

- Remember interesting, funny or clever things children say and do during the day and take a moment to share them with parents at the end of the day.

4. *Provide opportunities for parents to connect with their children's program experiences*

- Host an annual open house to familiarize families with your program. If possible, provide child-care services as an encouragement for families to attend.

- Offer periodic orientation meetings for families who join your program throughout the year. Set a regular schedule for orientations so that parents have an opportunity to participate within a few weeks of their child's entry into the program. Informal orientations can be offered as breakfast or after-work sessions. If possible, make child care available during orientation meetings.

- Publish a regular parent newsletter (once or twice a month) that contains information about planned activities, field trips, special events, quotes and stories by the children, and other news about the program that would be interesting and useful to parents. Consider having children help with the newsletter. See *Ideas for Parent Newsletters* in **Section Two** for more suggestions on creating parent newsletters.

- Invite parents to meet briefly with you after their child has been enrolled for a few weeks. Share examples of what children do in the program, encourage parents to ask questions and invite parent suggestions and participation in the program. Acknowledge that parents know their children better than anyone else and encourage them to share their knowledge with you. Conduct follow-up conferences with parents to share observations of children's development at least once a year.

- Have each child assemble a portfolio with samples of his/her work and play. In the portfolio, include artwork, photos of children involved in program activities, poems written by children, other writing samples, etc. Share portfolios with parents periodically. If a video camera is available, videotape children's participation in activities and loan the tape to parents to help them get a close look at what the program is like.

- Invite parents to participate in program activities (field trips, clubs, special activities related to their interests and talents).

- Invite parents to help you locate resources to support program activities (recyclable materials, people with talents and skills to share, etc.)

- Invite parents to make recordings of themselves reading, singing or talking to their child. Make the recordings available to children during the day.

- Invite parents to share family traditions by coming in to cook family recipes with the children, sending in photos of family celebrations or trips, helping plan a special program event related to their cultural traditions, etc.

- Encourage interested children to keep an illustrated journal of what they do each day. Remind children to share their journals with parents periodically.

5. *General ideas for helping parents feel welcome, accepted and valued*

- Work with the children to plan and host a Parent Appreciation Day (or night or week). Children can make special badges for their parents to wear all day, cook a special meal or snack, make "warm fuzzy" gifts, perform songs and skits, etc.

- Write personal notes to parents when they help out in some way. When appropriate, extend a public "thank you" in your parent newsletter or on the parent bulletin board.

- Inform parents well in advance of any policy or procedural changes that will affect them (changes in hours or days of operation, parking procedures, fees, etc.). Eliminate unpleasant surprises!

Ideas for Helping Parents Get to Know Program Staff

Ideas to get you started ...

1. *Provide parents with information about program staff*

   - Display close-up photos of staff involved in a favorite program activity (or engaged in a favorite hobby or pastime). Select pictures that clearly show faces, so they are easily recognizable for parents. Create informal biographies or autobiographies that include information about each staff person's education, experience, skills and talents. Emphasize information that relates directly to program activities as well as interests and hobbies that staff enjoy on their own time. Keep the tone of each bio informal and friendly. Clearly post the name each staff person likes to be called next to the photos and bios. (Information should be appropriate to share with parents and children.)

   - Publish a special edition of your program newsletter, featuring staff photos and biographies or autobiographies.

   - Feature a photo and brief autobiography of one staff member in each issue of your program newsletter.

   - Publish brief articles by staff in your parent newsletter (articles on topics such as what staff like best about working in your program; how staff share hobbies, talents or skills with the children, etc.). Encourage parents to talk with staff about their reactions to the articles.

   - Mount staff photos and brief bios or quotes in a scrapbook or photo album. Display the album in your parent comfort corner or near the entrance where parents come and go.

2. *Help parents identify staff members*

   - Have each staff member take the initiative to introduce himself/herself to each parent in the program. In addition to names, introductions might include titles, roles that staff play in the program and hobbies and activities the staff person enjoys sharing with the children.

   - Have staff wear easy-to-read name tags (especially at times of the year when many new families have been enrolled or at times when staff themselves are new).

   - Create a large mobile featuring photos and names of staff members. Display it near the entrance to the program.

- For larger programs, consider having staff wear brightly colored shirts embroidered with the program logo or name. This helps parents distinguish staff from volunteers and visiting parents and makes it easier for parents to know whom to approach for help, etc.

- Post staff photos and bios on the program Web site.

3. *Provide opportunities for parents and staff to work together and to interact informally*

   - Plan family events where parents, staff and children have opportunities to socialize informally (pizza parties, potluck suppers, bowling, hiking, camping, etc.)

   - Have individual staff members and parents serve together on committees related to various aspects of the program (policy-making, fundraising, parent education, resource development, publicity, newsletter, etc.)

   - Sponsor regular sharing meetings (monthly or bi-monthly) where parents and staff discuss parent and staff ideas, suggestions and concerns.

   - Put on a staff/parent talent show for children in the program.

   - Invite individual parents to join with staff to plan and carry out a special program activity, club or project with the children — cooking, woodworking, weaving, model building, pine-car derby, kite flying, photography, etc.

Ideas for Giving Parents Opportunities to Help Shape the Program

Ideas to get you started ...

1. *Provide parents with opportunities to shape their children's experiences in the program*

   - Talk daily with parents to gather information about their children's changing needs, interests, abilities, skills and talents. Use this information to help you individualize the program for each child. Let parents know you value the information they provide and keep them informed about how you use this information to support and guide their children in the program.

   - Invite parents to share photos of children engaged in favorite family-time activities or samples of projects that children enjoy doing at home and might also like to do in the program.

   - Provide opportunities for parents to meet with you periodically to share ideas about how you can work together to enhance their children's experiences in the program.

   - Make yourself available to discuss parents' concerns about their children's experiences; let them know how you plan to respond to their concerns.

   - Stay informed about the interests, talents, skills and other resources that parents may have to offer. Invite parents to share these resources whenever possible and let them know how their contributions enrich and enhance their children's experiences.

2. *Provide parents with opportunities to contribute to the development of program policies*

   - Include parent representatives on a program board or program advisory group.

   - If your program is not structured to have a board or advisory group, consider creating an informal parent advisory group that meets periodically with you to discuss program policies, problems, ideas for new program services, etc. Solicit volunteers for the group and enlist their help in keeping other parents informed about your discussions. Work with parents to devise a system for rotating parents in and out of the group from month to month or year to year to ensure continuity and a fresh flow of ideas and energy.

   - Involve parents in helping you evaluate the program environment and activities. Provide parents with a checklist for this purpose.

   - Invite parents to serve as chairwomen or co-chairmen of important policy committees as appropriate with your administrative structure.

- Use a variety of techniques to solicit parent feedback and suggestions (formal and informal written surveys, telephone surveys, feedback forms and suggestion boxes). See sample tools for this purpose in **Section Two.**

- Keep parents informed about community issues and upcoming decisions that may have an impact on your program. Publicize open board meetings, government forums or public hearings on school-age child-care issues so parents can decide if and how they would like to participate.

- Encourage interested parents to write letters in support of your program to legislators, newspaper opinion pages or other public opinion vehicles as needed.

- Always respond to parent suggestions and feedback. Even if you are not able to take actions that they have recommended, parents will appreciate knowing you have given their ideas serious consideration.

Ideas for Providing Parents with Opportunities to Get to Know Other Parents and Children in the Program

Ideas to get you started ...

1. *Provide parents with a place to gather in the program*

   Parents in your program need a place to chat and get to know each other. Refer to the tip sheet *Ideas for Helping Parents Feel Welcome, Accepted and Valued* that describes how to set up a parent comfort corner. Parents who have a special place to gather in the program are much more likely to get to know one another than parents who must snatch opportunities to talk with other parents as they pass in the hallway or get in and out of their cars.

2. *Assume the role of "social director" from time to time*

   Stay tuned in to the common needs, interests and concerns of parents and children. Take the opportunity to introduce them to one another when it seems appropriate. A few examples of parents who could benefit by being introduced to one another:

   • Parents whose children enjoy playing together in the program

   • Parents whose children share similar interests, skills or talents

   • Parents who work in the same area of town

   • Parents whose workplace experiences are similar

   • Parents who live in the same neighborhood who might like to share transportation responsibilities

   • Parents who share similar hobbies or recreational interests

3. *Sponsor family social events on a regular basis*

   In addition to helping parents get to know staff, family social events provide a great opportunity for parents to get to know other parents and children in the program in a relaxed atmosphere. Many programs offer family events every month or every other month. Listed below are some examples of family social events that are popular with families in school-age programs. Many of them can be combined to make one social event. Schedule events at the most convenient time for parents.

   • Potluck dinners — parents provide homemade or healthful "fast food" dinners.

   • Pizza parties — the program provides the food (purchased pizzas or pizzas made by the children) or families bring their favorite pizzas to share.

- Taste of the program — children prepare their favorite dishes and set up "booths" for parents to sample them.

- Continental breakfast socials — the program provides coffee, doughnuts, muffins, juice, etc., or parents volunteer to take turns providing the pastries.

- Talent shows — performances by children and/or parents and staff.

- Picnic and game festival — program provides drinks and supplies; parents bring a picnic food to share. After the meal, parents children, and staff play some of the program's favorite games together (cooperative games, competitive games, "wacky" games like water balloon toss, etc.). Several games may go on at the same time in different locations.

- Performances of original plays by the children

- Roller skating or ice skating parties — at a commercial rink or public park.

- Camping experiences, hiking and/or canoe trips — many programs make these two-day overnight events.

- Mini mall night — children create mini storefronts and display items they have made for sale. A mini food court serving drinks and snacks prepared by the children can be part of the mall. **Option:** Issue each family "play money" they can use to purchase items on sale in the "stores."

- Art gallery night — children create an art gallery of work they have done over several months and host an exhibit. Children prepare a program that lists artists and titles of their work. Special snacks are prepared and served by the cooking club.

- Inventor's Night — Parents and children work and play together to create "wacky inventions," using scrap materials. At the end of the night, families demonstrate their inventions (or other families try to guess what the inventions are supposed to do).

- White elephant auction night — each family contributes a usable item (or a mystery object) from their house that they no longer want. One parent serves as a "goofy" auctioneer and others bid on the treasures until all are sold. Proceeds can go to the parent comfort corner or to purchase an item for the program.

4. *Reserve a section of your parent bulletin board to make it easy for parents to recognize and contact each other*

   - Invite parents to post their business cards as a resource for other parents.

   - Encourage parents to post "help wanted" notes on the parent bulletin board. (For example, requests for help with transportation on days that parents must work overtime, requests for someone to share pickup responsibilities, invitations to other parents who might want to form a babysitting co-op, etc.)

   - Include photographs and brief bios of your families on the parent bulletin board. Include all families or feature one or more families each week. For more ideas, see *Ideas For Parent Bulletin Boards and Web Sites* in **Section Two.**

5. *Organize parent seminars and focus groups*

   Seminars and focus groups can provide parents with opportunities to network and share problems and solutions on topics of mutual interest and concern. Select topics based on your observations and conversations with parents and parent comments appearing on parent survey and feedback forms. Depending on staff knowledge and experience, seminars and focus groups may be led by staff or by outside experts on the topic. Examples of typical topics of interest to parents of school-age children:

   - How to communicate effectively with your children

   - How to guide children's behavior as they become more independent

   - How to set appropriate limits for children's behavior

   - How to handle bullying

   - How to help your child deal with peer pressure and/or sibling rivalry

   - How to guide your child's television watching, use of the Internet and electronic games

   - How to help your child learn about money (spending, saving, giving, investing)

   - How to get your child involved in helping out at home

   - How to use family meetings to keep the family working together

   - How to manage the challenges of being a single parent

   - How to help your child solve problems and conflicts

   - How to handle anger in children

6. *Establish a Family Resource and Energy Exchange (FREE) Network*

The FREE Network is designed to help parents connect by sharing various kinds of resources. Parents can save money by exchanging resources such as outgrown children's clothing, toys and games that children no longer use, household items, etc. Items no longer needed by one family may be just the thing another family is looking for. One of the main goals of the network is to make it possible for parents to exchange items at no charge. Anyone who contributes items to the network may take out items contributed by others. In addition to exchanging clothing or toys, the network can also provide a network for creating support networks (babysitting co-ops, telephone chains and ride exchanges for use in emergencies). Other uses of the network might be to help parents exchange ideas (for example, favorite recipes, birthday party ideas) or services (for example, cake baking, flower arranging, car washing, assembling toys or furniture, etc.). Some suggestions for organizing a FREE Network:

- Recruit two or three parents to help set up the FREE Network and determine operating policies and procedures. Encourage these parents to play a major role in the ongoing management of the network.

- Survey parents to determine what of items and/or services they are interested in exchanging. Start your FREE Network with the most popular items and services; add others as you go along.

- Determine operating policies and procedures. (Keep policies and procedures as simple as possible so that parents will find the network easy to use.) For example:

  - Will contributed items need to be stored or will there be a designated time each month when items can be contributed and taken out? How and when will you dispose of unclaimed items? (Give away to another organization? Contribute to the school-age program?)

  - If storage space is a problem, could you develop a "catalog" listing items and services that parents have contributed, rather than having items brought to the program?

  - How many items or units of service do parents need to contribute in order to use the network? Will value be assigned to items and services? Or, if parents contribute a minimum number of items or units of service, will they be allowed to use any of the network services for a specified time? Will you issue credits or coupons to contributing parents to "spend" in the network?

  - Will ongoing records of donations and exchanges be monitored?

- Set aside one area of the parent bulletin board to publicize the FREE Network. Also, include stories about the network in your parent newsletter.

Ideas for Helping Parents Support Their Child's School Success

Staff in school-age programs play an important role in helping children make a smooth transition from home to school and from school to home. When school-age staff, parents and schools work together as partners, children are more likely to experience success in school. It is important for school-age staff to recognize that they are in a position to serve as important communication links between parents and school and vice versa.

It is also important for school-age staff to recognize that there are many ways to support children's school success during program hours. Before school, parents count on school-age staff to involve children in appropriate morning activities and help them get ready for a great school day. At the end of the school day, parents count on school-age staff to give children a warm welcome, assess their well-being, find out how the day went and help them get positively and productively involved in appropriate program activities. Here are some things school-age staff can do to strengthen partnerships among schools, parents and school-age programs to help parents support their child's school success.

Ideas to get you started ...

1. *Talk with school personnel/classroom teachers to explore ways you can work together to create a smooth transition for children from home to the program to school and back again.*

    *   Identify challenges that can impact communication between the home, school and the program and share ideas for addressing those challenges.

    *   Consult *Homework Assistance & Out-of-School Time: Filling the Need and Finding the Balance* for ideas on addressing challenging communication issues. (See **Selected References** at the end of this book.)

    *   Offer to set up home/school folders for each child. (See Number 2 below.)

    *   Ask if there are ways you could support children's school success in the program. (For example, giving children homework reminders, reviewing homework assignments with children, building on themes introduced in the school day, checking homework assignments posted by teachers on a school Web site and encouraging children to apply what they're learning in school during program activities.)

2. *Set up a Home/School Folder for each child*

    *   Use the folder to keep homework assignment notebooks, completed homework, notes from the child's teacher to the parents, notes from the parents to the child's teacher, etc.

    *   Set up an area where children store their Home/School Folders during program hours.

- Develop a system where children deposit home/school folders on arrival and pick them up when they leave the program. If children do homework in the program, have them take the home/school folder to the homework area and return it to the central area when they are finished.

3. *In cases where children need special help and support, develop a system where school staff and program staff can share information about the child's needs and the best ways to help the child.* Be sure to secure parent permission in writing before information is shared.

4. *Survey parents to learn about their interests in having children do homework during the program.* Or discuss homework issues at a parent meeting. Consult *Homework Assistance & Out-of-School Time: Filling the Need and Finding the Balance* for ideas on creating a survey format. Keep in mind that different parents have different levels of interest in having programs provide homework support — ranging from wanting tutorial help for their children to preferring their children not do homework in the program.

5. *Once you know more about parents' interests, work with colleagues to develop a homework policy that allows you to address parents' needs in the best ways possible within your program guidelines.*

   - Determine the extent to which your current staff is equipped to provide homework support. Provide staff training on effective techniques for giving homework support. Explore the possibility of securing additional staff support, if needed.

   - Try to create a homework policy that meets diverse needs, rather than taking a one-size-fits-all approach. For example, avoid creating a plan where all children must do homework in the same place at the same time for a specified period, regardless of how much homework a child was assigned for the day. Instead, create a plan that allows children to select when they will do homework and for how long, based on what they need to accomplish. The use of a homework agreement/contract between a child, parent, classroom teacher and school-age staff can serve as a tool for individualizing the approach to homework support for each child and family. A contract can allow staff to accommodate differences among parents as well as differences related to children's ages and homework responsibilities. See *Homework Assistance & Out-of-School Time: Filling the Need and Finding the Balance* for ideas on different approaches to providing homework support.

6. *Set up an attractive homework interest center stocked with a lot of supplies and equipment to make it easy to do homework.* Select an area that is a little removed from other interest areas, if possible. Give the area a catchy name like Homework Haven. Create an inviting atmosphere that makes children want to visit the center to work on learning activities, whether they have homework or not. If your program operates in shared space, use plastic bins, rolled carts and rolled shelving units to store and display items. Involve children in helping to set up the area each day. Some things to incorporate when creating a homework area:

- pencils with erasers, colored pencils, ballpoint pens, fine-point markers, different types of paper, file folders, tape, glue, scissors, dictionaries, a variety of resource books, magazines, atlas, encyclopedia, an assortment of educational games, calculators, computer station(s) and computer software to assist with researching projects, printer and other school-related supplies

- small tables with chairs or benches, filing cabinet, shelving for books and educational games, bulletin board(s) and floor or table lamps to soften lighting

- room dividers to separate different areas of the homework area if the area is large (for example, you may want to separate an area for group work on projects from an area where children work alone without conversation)

- individual table-top study carrels (mini dividers) to minimize distractions when children are seated together at a table, but need to work alone (can be homemade from recycled cardboard — tape three sections into a U shape for privacy and have each child decorate his/her own)

- comfortable chairs, large pillows, fire retardant rugs and/or other cozy items where children can sit and relax while they read and think

7. *Provide parents with information on current research related to homework, the purpose of homework, homework do's and don'ts, etc.*

   - Post results of research on your parent bulletin board.

   - Prepare articles about homework for your parent newsletter.

   - To learn more about research on homework, consult books related to homework listed in the **Selected References** at the end of this book.

8. *Provide staff with additional training related to staff roles in giving homework help. Consult books related to homework listed in* **Selected References**.

Ideas for Advocating on Behalf of Parents and Families

Most of the relationship-building ideas and tips in **Section Three** relate to things that staff can do as they work directly with parents to initiate and build relationships with parents and families. Staff also can strengthen relationships with parents by assuming an advocacy role with others on behalf of parents and families. **Note:** Be sure to discuss your role as an advocate with your supervisor or director before developing and acting on your personal advocacy plan. Here are some ideas for playing an advocacy role.

Ideas to get you started ...

1. *Stay informed about local, state and national legislation related to child-care and family-support issues.*

   - Attend public hearings on these issues

   - Join with your colleagues to speak up in support of issues you think are beneficial to families

   - Speak out against initiatives that you believe would be harmful to families

   - Write letters to your representatives in legislative and executive branches to encourage their support of family-friendly policies and actions

2. *Maintain a close watch on the policies and procedures of your own program to ensure they are fair and supportive of the families you serve.* Even if you are not in the role of decision maker, respectfully share your perspectives on important issues that can impact families with those who do make decisions. This might include issues such as program hours, days of operation, registration procedures, affordability, fee structure, and fee collection. The perspectives of staff who work directly with parents and families can provide valuable insights to those who make policy decisions. Remember, it is possible to provide leadership from within an organization by participating in the discussion of important issues.

3. *Join professional and/or advocacy organizations (locally, statewide and/or national) that promote access to quality child care and other out-of-school services for families.* Participate in campaigns and initiatives sponsored by the organization(s). See **Selected References** for names of national organizations.

4. *Look for opportunities to partner with other organizations to initiate and operate jointly sponsored programs and services that benefit children and families.* (For example, a partnership between your program and a local sports league; an arts studio; a community health center; a recreation center; a police department drug prevention program; a business that could provide scholarships or other funding to reduce costs for parents.)

5. *Write letters to the editor of your local newspaper in support of local initiatives to strengthen families.* (For example, initiatives that provide free or low-cost access to school and community facilities for after-school programs and other out-of-school services; initiatives that subsidize the cost of child-care services for needy and low- and moderate-income families; initiatives that expand services for underserved populations, such as children with special needs.)

6. *Make a concerted effort to be aware of the needs, stresses and pressures on families in your program and in your community.*

   • When you know a family is in crisis (for example, their home is destroyed in a fire or flood, a parent is killed in an auto accident, a single parent suddenly loses his/her job), join with other colleagues and program managers to explore how you can create a support network that will help the family through the crisis.

   • Remember that advocacy is not limited to political action; it also includes compassion and caring for individuals in need.

Building and Sustaining Positive Relationships with Parents

(Article adapted and excerpted from Roberta L. Newman, Keys to Quality in School-Age Child Care)

Unless we make a continuing effort to build and sustain positive relationships with parents, parents must depend on their children for information and use their imaginations to fill in the blanks. Some parents imagine everything is wonderful when really it is not. Other parents are nervous about what they do not know and sometimes imagine the worst. Based on very little information, they may develop a negative impression about the quality of their children's experiences. Still, other parents may feel confused about what's going on and what kind of role they can play in their child's school-age program.

When their children are not with them, parents want to know what and how they are doing. Parents like to hear about the little things their children say and do — anecdotes about daily happenings that give them insights about how their children see the world. They also want to know when children are having problems (even though their initial reaction can be negative or defensive at times).

Ongoing, good communication between parents and child-care professionals is essential if we hope to make a positive difference in the lives of school-age children. Three steps you can take to ensure that ongoing positive communication can take place between you and the parents you serve are:

1. *Share Information*

   Set up formal ways for parents to learn about daily and weekly happenings in your program. Start out right. Think through what types of orientation materials parents need: policy and procedure statements; health and safety guidelines; program philosophy and standards; and descriptions of the daily schedule of activities. Once children are attending your program, keep the information coming. Use parent bulletin boards, calendars of events and regular newsletters to keep parents up-to-date on program happenings.

   Remember that sharing information implies a two-way exchange of information. Find out about children's needs and interests and parent needs and expectations through daily chats, conferences, suggestion boxes and parent surveys. Offer discussion groups where parents can clarify their understanding of the program and explore ways the program can better meet the needs of children and parents.

   Communicate regularly about each child's experience in the program. Take time to send home "good news" notes or make a short phone call when a child learns a new skill, solves a hard problem, makes something beautiful, says something funny or has an especially happy day.

2. *Develop a plan for building relationships*

Communication experts tell us that the more we talk to one another, the more positive our attitude toward communicating can become. Brief exchanges between child-care professionals and parents at drop-off and pick-up times help build open, friendly relationships. Daily warm greetings and good-byes help children and parents feel comfortable and important.

In addition to informal daily chats, plan opportunities for parents to be involved in your program so you can get to know each other. Invite parents to attend special program activities such as songfests, talent shows, visits from local musicians or other performers. Encourage parents to participate in field trips, if possible. Take photos and make videos of these events to share with parents who cannot attend. Invite parents to help with special projects such as repairing equipment at home or helping with a Saturday clean-up and repair day.

3. *Share problems when they occur*

Even if child care professionals work at building and sustaining relationships with parents, sharing problems is never easy. Yet, it can be one of the most important services we can provide as child-care professionals. While parents are often understandably apprehensive about discussing problems, they don't want to be kept in the dark. They want to know. How can school-age professionals meet the challenge of sharing problems or concerns with parents in the most effective way? A few suggestions:

- *Share problems at the right time and in the right place.* When you have genuine concerns, never share them casually or in front of other people. Plan thoughtfully and set up a private meeting (or a private phone call if a meeting is not possible). Keep in mind that it is often difficult for parents and school-age professionals to focus productively on problem sharing and problem solving at the end of a long work day when they may feel emotionally, mentally and physically drained.

- *Start a problem-sharing conversation by offering some positive comments first.* Remember what Haim Ginott said in his book *Teacher and Child*, "When a teacher talks to parents about their children, he inevitably intrudes on family dreams." Also, end your meeting with positive comments, if at all possible.

- *When describing a problem, be factual and objective.* Avoid preaching, blaming, criticizing or judging (the child or the parent).

- *Monitor the reactions of parents.* As you talk with parents about problems, maintain relaxed eye contact and be aware of body language or words that indicate the parent my be feeling tense, hurt, disappointed or angry.

- *Ask questions, get advice and invite parents to work with you.* Remember that parents know their children better than anyone else. Find out if they have the same perspective and expectations of their children that you do. Work toward creating strategies for solving the problem that are mutually acceptable to the parent, the child and you. Stress the importance of consistency between home and the school-age program.

- *Listen.* When you solicit comments and suggestions from parents, be sure to listen to what they have to say. Keep these listening guidelines in mind:

  - Be genuinely open to hearing ideas and opinions. Take time to hear parents out. Don't interrupt. Don't rush.

  - Acknowledge and reflect parent's feelings. Be willing to accept feelings even if they're different from your own. Check your perceptions of parents' feelings and opinions by restating what you have understood them to say.

  - Trust parents' abilities to find solutions to problems. Let them know you value them as a resource.

Always remember that productive two-way communication supports the development and maintenance of positive relationships that are always in the best interests of children. Positive relationships never develop by accident. They take thoughtful planning as well as constant nurturing and attention.

Selected References

General Communication and Building Relationships

Heller, Robert. *Communicating Clearly*. New York, NY: DK Publishing, 1998.

McKay, Matthew, PH.D.; Davis, Martha, Ph.D.; Fanning, Patrick. *How to Communicate: The Ultimate Guide to Improving Your Personal and Professional Relationships*. 2nd Edition. New York, NY: MJF Books, Fine Communications, 1995.

Stone, Douglas; Patton, Bruce; Heen, Sheila. *Difficult Conversations: How to Discuss What Matters Most*. New York, NY: Viking Press, 1999.

Homework Issues and Supporting School Success

Homework and Edutainment Program, Video and Companion Guide. Boston, MA: Produced by The Activities Club and WFD Consulting, 2002. Available from WFD Consulting, 55 Chapel Street, Newton, MA 02458 (617-219-8700)

Kohn, Alfie. *The Case Against Homework*. Portsmouth, NH: Heineman, 2000.

Kohn, Alfie. *The Homework Myth: Why Our Kids Get Too Much of a Bad Thing*. Da Capo Books, 2006.

O'Connor, Susan, and McGuire, Kate. *Homework Assistance & Out-of-School Time: Filling the Need, Finding a Balance* (published with Hynes, Kathryn, O'Connor, Susan, and Chung, An-Me. *Literacy: Exploring Strategies to Enhance Learning in After-School Programs*). Wellesley, MA: NIOST and New Albany, OH: School-Age NOTES, 2001. (Note: Also available from NIOST: *Homework and Out-of-School Time: Filling the Need, Finding a Balance*. This is a summary of the book published as a booklet). National Institute on Out-of-School Time (NIOST).

Links to Learning: A Curriculum Planning Guide for After-School Programs. Wellesley, MA: NIOST and New Albany, OH: School-Age NOTES, 2004.

Parenting and Sharing Information with Parents

Galinsky, Ellen. *The Six Stages of Parenthood*. Reading, MA: Perseus Books, 1987.

Newman, Roberta. *Creating Portfolios with Kids in Out-of-School Programs: IDEAs for Communicating with Parents and Enhancing Program Quality*. Cape Charles, VA: Newroads Media, 2005.

Ginott, Haim. *Between Parent and Child*. Revised and updated by Alice Ginott and Dr. H. Wallace Goddard. New York, NY: Three Rivers Press, 2003.

Ginott, Haim. *Teacher and Child*. Touchstone Publishers, 1998.

Gordon, Thomas. *Parent Effectiveness Training: The Proven Program for Raising Responsible Children*. New York, NY: Three Rivers Press, 2000.

Professional and Advocacy Organizations

Note: *There are numerous professional and advocacy organizations that provide information and services useful to staff in school-age programs and other out-of-school time services. Some of the most prominent of these organizations are listed on the following pages. Search the Internet to find additional organizations related to specific interests and concerns for children and families during out-of-school time.*

National AfterSchool Association (NAA) (a professional organization for the after-school field, offers an annual conference and publishes a professional journal)
529 Main Street, Suite 214
Charlestown, MA 02129
800-617-8242
617-778-6020
www.naaweb.org

Afterschool Alliance (an advocacy organization dedicated to promoting availability of after-school services to all children and families through state-wide and national initiatives)
1616 H St., NW
Washington, DC 20006
(202) 347-2030
www.afterschoolalliance.org

Association for Childhood Education International (ACEI) (focused on the care and education of children from birth through adolescence; publishes a newsletter, research journal and books).
17904 Georgia Avenue, Suite 215
Olney, MD 20832
(800) 423-3563
www.acei.org

Academy for Educational Development (focused on youth development and promoting promising practices to provide youth with effective services)
1825 Connecticut Avenue, NW
Washington, DC 20009-5721
(202) 884-8000
www.aed.org

Harvard Family Research Project (HFRP) (focused on helping philanthropies, policymakers and practitioners promote the educational and social success and well-being of children, families and communities)
Harvard Graduate School of Education
3 Garden Street
Cambridge, MA 02138
(617) 495-9108
www.gse.harvard.edu/hfrp

National Black Child Development Institute (NBCDI) (dedicated to improving the quality of life for black children and families)
1313 L Street, NW, Suite 110
Washington, DC 20005
(202) 833-2220
www.nbcdi.org

National Community Education Association (NCEA) (promotes the idea that educational resources of a community should be available to learners of all ages and educational backgrounds; publishes a quarterly journal)
3929 Old Lee Highway, Suite 91-A
Fairfax, VA 22030
(703) 359-8973
www.ncea.com

National Institute on Out-of-School Time (NIOST) (a national research and training organization focused on out-of-school time opportunities for children and youth; publishes research reports, studies, position papers and books)
Wellesley Centers for Women at Wellesley College
106 Central Street
Wellesley, MA 02481
(781) 283-2547
www.niost.org

National Latino Children's Institute (NLCI) (an advocate for the welfare and healthy development of Latino children; conducts public education campaigns and has a resource center)
1115 S. St. Mary's Street
San Antonio, TX 78210
(210) 228-9997
www.nlci.org

National Parent Teacher Association (largest volunteer child-advocacy organization)

PTA National Headquarters
541 N. Fairbanks Court
Suite 1300
Chicago, IL 60611
(312) 670-6782
www.pta.org

PTA Office of Programs and Public Policy
1400 L Street, NW
Suite 300
Washington, DC 20005
(202) 289-6790
www.pta.org

Roberta L. Newman has extensive experience as a director, trainer and developer of training and curriculum materials for out-of-school programs. As a program director of a large multi-site school-age care program, she founded a program-wide parent advisory group and parent newsletter and initiated a broad range of programs designed to build positive relationships with families. In recent years, she has helped out-of-school programs across the country create innovative ways to work with parents as active partners. Roberta's experiences with diverse out-of-school programs resulted in this book for trainers and practitioners who are committed to making positive connections with parents and families.

Also by Roberta L. Newman:

Keys to Quality in School-Age Care (video and training guides)

Caring for Children in School-Age Programs, with Derry Koralek and Laura Colker

Training New After-School Staff

I.D.E.A.s – Integrated Developmental Enhancement Activities:
Creating Successful Out-of-School Experiences in Programs for Older Children and Youth

Creating Portfolios with Kids in Out-of-School Programs

Connect with Music: IDEAS for Creating Music Experiences with Kids in Out-of-School Programs

Pay Attention: Answers to Common Questions about the Diagnosis and Treatment of Attention Deficit Disorder, with Craig B. Liden, MD; Jane Reck and Mary Wolowicz

Helping Children and Youth with ADD Succeed in After-School Programs

School-Age Activity Packs: Dollars and Kid Sense, Communication Connections, and Get Fit

Would you like to have Roberta Newman lead a workshop on Building Relationships with Parents and Families for directors, trainers or staff in your program or community? For information on how to arrange a one- or two-day session, contact Roberta:

Roberta Newman — Newroads Consulting
(a division of Cape Charles Development Co.)

Eight Randolph Avenue

Cape Charles, VA 23310

Telephone: 757-331-3151

FAX: 757-331-4474

E-mail: Newroads_Consulting@earthlink.net

Visit Roberta's Web Site: www.Newroads-Consulting.com

Building Relationships with Parents and Families in School-Age Programs
CD enhancement

School-Age NOTES is pleased to offer selected handouts from Roberta Newman's *Building Relationships with Parents and Families in School-Age Programs*.

The CD features more than 40 pages of Core Learning Activity handouts plus sample posters for promoting a family-friendly program environment, and sample cover letters and response forms from *Building Relationships* for only $9.95.

This CD provides a convenient way to print and distribute these handouts plus easy access for multiple copies. When combined with *Building Relationships*, the handouts on this CD work together to create a valuable training tool for you and your staff.

To order this CD for $9.95 (plus shipping and handling), go to www.SchoolAgeNotes.com or call School-Age NOTES at 614-855-9315.

If you enjoyed this book, consider purchasing others by Roberta Newman and those published by School-Age NOTES.

School-Age NOTES is a proven provider of practical resources in areas such as:

- administration & training
- tools for trainers
- creating environments
- guidance & discipline
- cooking & nutrition
- creative arts
- cultural diversity
- enrichment
- fitness & games
- life skills
- music & drama
- middle school
- high school
- summer

School-Age NOTES is a trusted provider of innovative resources for after-school professionals.

Go to www.SchoolAgeNotes.com to see our full line of resources or call 614-855-9315 to request a catalog.